Early Childhood and Elementary Education

Early Childhood and Elementary Education

ISMAIL THAMARASSERI

KANISHKA PUBLISHERS, DISTRIBUTORS
NEW DELHI-110 002

KANISHKA PUBLISHERS, DISTRIBUTORS
4697/5-21A, Ansari Road, Daryaganj
New Delhi -110 002
Phones : 2327 0497, 2328 8285
Fax : 011-2328 8285
E-mail : kanishka_publishing@yahoo.co.in

Early Childhood and Elementary Education
Edition: 2016

PRINTED IN INDIA

Published by Madan Sachdeva for Kanishka Publishers, Distributors, 4697/5-21A, Ansari Road, Daryaganj, New Delhi-110 002, Typeset by Sunshine Graphics, Delhi, and Printed at Rajdhani Printers, Delhi.

PREFACE

Education is a critical input in human resource development and is essential for the countries economic growth. The need and importance of early childhood education is now being recognised all over the world. The child acquired most of its personal and social habits before the age of six. Early years of the child are plastic and impressionable. It is during these years that the bases for later development are laid. Recent development in the field of psychology have focused the attention of the society on the needs of children during the impressionable years.

This book couldn't have been written without contribution from a number of people and I am indebted to each of them for their support and encouragement. I am indebted to the various authors, research scholars, and educationists whose views and opinions have been incorporated in the text, the names of which have been duly incorporated in the bibliographies given towards the end of the work. The author expresses his gratitude to the writers and publishers of these works. The author shall ever remain obliged to his teachers, parents, friends, family members, students, teacher trainees, colleagues for their directions and guidance. The author is also great thankful to M/s. Infratec Computer Systems, Calicut University for the Computerisation of the work. To them all, the author offers his greatful thanks to M/s. Kanishka Publishers, Distributors, New Delhi who came forward willingly to undertake the publishing of this book at a short time.

ISMAIL THAMARASSERI

Kottakkal, Kerala
16th April 2008

CONTENTS

1
Introduction

The Scope and Need of Early Childhood Education

A number of social factors have contributed to the expansion of early childhood programmes and brought early childhood education into the public consciousness. These include:

- Changes in family life such as an increased number of two-earner families and single parents.
- Growing evidence of the benefits of early education for children from poverty, children with disabilities, and other children at risk.
- Child advocacy, which has helped bring the needs of young children and their families to public and legislatives prominence.

There is considerable diversity in the types of early childhood programmes with variations according to:

- Purpose of programmes
- Programme settings
- Ages of the children
- Sources of funding support

A most important factor in describing early childhood programmes is quality. The following elements contribute to the quality of early childhood programmes:

- Child-adult ratio
- Group size

- Mixed-age grouping
- Developmental appropriateness of the programme
- Quality of adult-child interaction
- Staff qualification
- Staff consistency
- Respect and concern for the staff
- Quality of the physical environment
- Family involvement
- Quality as a combination of factors

There are trends and projections that suggest what the future holds for early childhood education.

The Children

Young children are alike in three common areas:

- "Profiles" that identify typical traits shared by the majority of children of different ages.
- The need of all children for positive self-esteem
- The need of all children for play as a way of learning about the world
- Factors that contribute to the wonderful diversity among children include inborn traits and external factors.

Some children have specific, special needs that make them unique. The early childhood programme can help meet the needs of special children by:

- The inclusion of disabled and non disabled children into the same programme.
- Recognising characteristics of children with motor, cognitive, learning, visual, hearing, communication, emotional and health problems, as well as gifted children.

The Families

Family system theory is a way of viewing the family as a dynamic unit.

The family has undergone many changes recently. Consider some of these changes by looking at the following:

- Variety in family forms

- Other factors that contribute to family diversity
- Families in poverty

Families have specific needs that the early childhood programme can address. Consider issues related to family needs, including;

- The needs of adults in a unique stage of development, separate from their children's development.
- The need to feel empowered, in control of their lives.
- Coordination of the needs of the family with the early childhood programme.

Two-way communication between families and the early childhood programme is an important element in providing consistency for children. Consider the following methods of communicating with parents:

- Communicating with individual parents informally, on a day-to-day basis, and formally, through conferences and home visits.
- Communicating with groups of parents, through written communiqués, bulletin boards, and meetings.

Families can be involved in the early childhood programme in a number of ways-as resources, in the classroom, and as decision makers.

One function of the early childhood programme is parent education, which can take a variety of forms.

The Who of Early Childhood Education

Early childhood teacher can be described by some identifiable personal qualities. Consider some predictable stages in their development. The staffs of early childhood programmes can be include a number of individuals in a variety of roles, including the director, teaching staff, volunteers, support staff, board of directors and community professionals. A variety of training possibilities and regulating entities are associated with early childhood programmes.

- Early childhood teachers might receive training through academic channels or through the Child Development Associate programme.
- Early childhood programmes are licensed through local or state regulations, which set minimum standards.

- Many programmes undergo voluntary accreditation through the National Academy of Early Childhood Programmes.

Professionalism in early childhood education is noted by such criteria as a code of ethics and the existence of professional organisations. Although early childhood education presents you with exciting challenges, as a student entering this career, it also presents some issues and dilemmas:

- Some of the problems faced by early childhood educators are rooted in the historic antecedents of the field.
- Early childhood education faces some serious concerns, including teacher shortage, low pay, burnout, and scarcity of men in the field.
- Through advocacy and empowerment of early childhood professional, these issues are beginning to be addressed.

The Why of Early Childhood Education

Early childhood education, although relatively new as a formal system, has antecedents that reach far back in history as ideas about children and how they should be treated were shaped. The writings and work of many individuals through history have contributed to our contemporary ideas about young children and early childhood education. Particularly in this century, a number of theorists have proposed models that help us understand the nature of young children and how best to meet their needs.

- Some theorists believe that children's development follows an inborn plan.
- Others consider that children's development is affected primarily by external factors.

Many theories have been applied to early childhood education through the development of specific programme models. Research has proven the effectiveness of early education.

Goals provide an overall, general overview of what is expected of the children. Objectives are a more specific interpretation of goals. There are different type of objectives. Evaluation is an important element in early childhood education and helps assess whether goals and objectives are being met.

- One of the most widely used methods of evaluation is observation
- Teacher-designed instruments such as checklists and ratings scales are another type of evaluation.
- Many commercially produced standardised tests are used for different purposes.
- Although evaluation instruments are widely used, there is also considerable concern about their use.
- Information from evaluation and assessments can be used in different ways.

The Where of Early Childhood Education

- The physical environment affects both children and adults.
- Consider the importance of the indoor environment, focusing on how to use it most effectively to support the development of young children.
- Consider the outdoor environment and how to maximise its potential.
- Occasionally the environment must be adapted to meet the requirements of children with special needs.
- Select developmentally appropriate equipment, with particular emphasis on the role of computers in early childhood programmes.
- Consider criteria for selecting appropriate material for use in early childhood programmes.

Scheduling and Curriculum Planning

- Look at the common components of the daily schedule in an early childhood programme.
- Examine some guidelines for setting an effective schedule.
- Whether a programme operates full-day or part-day will have an impact on the schedule and what it includes.
- The schedule should be consistent and predictable, but also flexible when needed.
- Consideration of curriculum includes both definition and examination of its elements.
  - *(i)* Curriculum needs to be directly related to the development of the children in the programme.
  - *(ii)* Curriculum must include relevant content to be appropriate.

- Consider the development of written plans, including the overall curriculum, units, daily lesson plans, and activities.

Creative Development Through the Curriculum

Consider the definition and discussion of some of the characteristics of creativity. Research on the different functions of the two sides of the brain is relevant to this discussion. Both the teacher's attitude and the physical environment are important in encouraging creativity in young children. One of the early childhood curriculum areas in which creativity can especially flourish is art.

- There are several theoretical views of the process of art.
- Many types of art activities and materials are appropriate in the early childhood classroom.
- Aesthetic appreciation is another element of art that can be nurtured in the early years.

A second broad curriculum area that fosters creativity is music. Consider listening to music, singing, playing musical instruments, and creative movements as they relate to children. Some factors discourage and decrease creativity, including television.

Physical Development Through the Curriculum

Consider the theories that explain physical development. Physical development is complex, involving a number of interrelated components.

- Body control involves mastering a number of skills important for movement and balance.
- Young children grain increasing manual control, the ability to use the hands effectively.
- Sensory-perceptual development involves children's increasing accuracy in interpreting information they gain through their senses.

Several early childhood activities encourage and promote use of the large muscles of the body.

- Physical fitness activities and outdoor play provide excellent opportunities for large muscle development.
- Consider the value of blocks and block play for young children.

Many manipulative materials and activities promote use and development of the small muscles of hands and fingers. Because of the importance of learning through the senses for young children, consider activities that promote sensory exploration and discrimination. A major aspect of physical development includes learning to care for the body, in relation to nutrition, health and safety.

Cognitive Development Through the Curriculum

There are three influential theoretical views of cognitive development: behaviourism, cognitive developmental theory, and information processing. Cognition begins to develop in earliest infancy, through movement and sensory experiences. During the pre-school years, children begin to acquire some specific cognitive skills.

- Consider five cognitive tasks–classification, seriation, number concepts, temporal concepts, and spatial concepts–and activities that can help children master them.
- Children also acquire a considerable amount of information during their early years.

Two important early childhood curriculum areas to consider are maths and science.

Language Development Through the Curriculum

There are several divergent theoretical views of language development. Some components of language can help us understand the complexity of all that children attain during their early years. Because many early childhood programmes include children who speak a language other than English, consider bilingualism and effective strategies for teaching children a second language. Many components of the early childhood programme support and reinforce language learning.

- Conversations and language play offer many spontaneous opportunities for language learning.
- Also consider some of the many types of planned activities aimed at enhancing language.
- Emergent literacy is children's ongoing process of learning, reading and writing.

The How of Early Childhood Education-Curriculum

Consider the theoretical views of how socialisation takes place. Consider the development of social competence.

- An important element in the development of social competence is peer interaction and friendships.
- Children also develop gender role identity; consider nonsexist teaching strategies that promote positive gender attitudes.
- Racial and cultural attitudes, and attitudes toward the disabled, are formed early in life; review guidelines that can help promote accepting attitudes towards others.
- The foundations for moral development and positive social skills and behaviours are also formed during the early years.

There are two types of activities that can promote positive social interaction, specifically, socio-dramatic play and cooperative games.

The How of Early Childhood Education-Guidance

Consider four routine times: arrival and departure, meals, toileting, and sleep. All four have strong emotional significance for the child and need sensitive handling by the teachers. Some important factors affect group behaviour, particularly the developmental appropriateness of expectations and activities. Forethought and planning can help ensure an orderly classroom during specific time blocks within the daily schedule. Transition, those time when children move from one activity to the next, deserve special attention. Consider occasions when the out-of-the-ordinary happens, either planned - such as a field trip-or unplanned-for instance, an accident.

Guiding Social Behaviours

Consider the kinds of behaviours we expect of children. Examine workable philosophies of guidance.

- These include the approaches of Rudolf Dreikurs, Thomas Gordon, and the behaviourists.
- Look at how to select a personal guidance approach.

Consider definitions and distinctions among words related to guidance and discipline. Look at a variety of guidance techniques and when these are used most effectively. Consider where to draw the line between behaviours that fall within the normal range and behaviours for which professional help should be sought. Consider the underlying causes of misbehaviour, factors that in both subtle and direct ways affect the way children behave. Two specific behavioural concerns, aggression and shyness, are of particular concern to many teachers.

Helping Children Cope with Stress

Define stress and coping and look at the stages of stress. A variety of possible sources for stress exist in young children's lives.

- Family stressors, including divorce, poverty and homelessness, and fast-placed family life, can have a serious effect on children.
- Child abuse and neglect, in addition to the potential for severe harm, is a serious source of stress for young children.
- Health problems and dealing with death are other stressful occurrences for children.

Children may have a wide variety of adverse effects from stress. The early childhood teacher can use a number of effective techniques to help children cope with the stress in their lives. Some programmes are designed to teach young children self-protection from potentially harmful encounters.

REFERENCE

1. Essa, E.L. *Introduction to Early Childhood Education* (3rd Ed.).

2

Need, Importance and Objectives of Early Childhood Education

Need and Importance

The child acquires most of its personal and social habits before the age of six. It is during these years that the bases for later development are laid. Recent developments in the field of psychology have focused the attention of the society on the needs of children during the impressionable years.

Early education has existed in many countries of the world for many years. But the recent findings in the area of cognitive development have lent on educational justification to what Evans has called 'early intervention'. Bloom (1964) has analyzed research data on growth of intelligence. It shows that 50 per cent of the total intellectual development of the child is completed by the time a child is four years old. Research in the area of creativity have also pointed out that if the children are provided early formalised experiences through play, their creative ability will also be enhanced.

Bloom (1964) in his book *Stability and Change in Human Characteristics* has analyzed data concerning intelligence which led him to conclude that the rate of intellectual development is at the point of highest acceleration during the child's early years. The greatest advantage in matters of child's intellectual development will come from the stimulation of home and school environment of the child during the first four to six year of life.

Need of the early educational experiences has been highlighted in a document entitled, Low Cost Day Provision for the Under-Fivers, (Britain Department of Education and Science, 1976).

"Young children need to acquire physical skills which demand muscular control and the development of fine and coordinated movement. They, therefore, need adequate indoor and out of door space and equipment, to provide opportunities for running, climbing, jumping, balancing building, manipulating small objects such as puzzles and constructional toys, modelling clay and though using scissors and point brush with increasing dexterity. The planned experiences of nursery education can help to develop increased awareness and the ability to appreciate and discriminate size and shape, order and progression, and movement and change" (p. 13).

The U.S. Research and Policy Committee for Economic Development (1971) observed, "pre-schooling is desirable for all children, but it is necessary for disadvantaged. Without it, these is little possibility of achieving equality in education .... Only a massive effort to establish both public and private pre-school educational programmes will provide the preparation in motivation, intellectual capacities and physical skills essential to success in achieving total basic literacy (pp. 35-37).

Sergeant (1969) said, "... No efforts should be spared to persude parents to send their children to school voluntarily where housing conditions are unsatisfactory and/or mothers are accustomed to go out to work" (p. 78).

The Central Advisory Board of the Government of India (January, 1944) observed, "It is one of the many consequences of the general lack of educational planning in India that a new impressionable plastic and educationally potent period of life has received so little attention."

Dr. Zakir Hussain (1955) said, "Ideas of inequality, still unfortunately persisting in society, can be more easily discarded by children well trained in early years... children brought up in special schools, from which the poor are excluded on principle or by poverty... the union and state governments can insist on every nursery school, new or old, reserving a certain percentage of places for children of the poor and providing them with ample facilities for fitting them into its "milieu". Such schools will have a high educative value for parents, too, who will learn to recognise the rich individuality and latent capacities of all children" (p. 51- Indore Report).

Why of Early Childhood Education

Muralidharan (1969) provided the following justification of nursery education in her book, *A guide for nursery school teachers.*

1. The rate of development of the child at the pre-school age (3-6 years) is so rapid that the child can be given more and more experiences.
2. There is tremendous wastage and stagnation in India in class I and II.
3. The change in the family system, i.e. in case of mothers going work, the provision of nursery education is a social and economic necessity.
4. The urbanisation, forming of slums, and increasing density of population leads to in adequacy of child's play and out door activities. Nursery schools can take care of the child's needs.
5. The nursery schools can provide guidance to the parents for the bringing up of their children or more sound footing.
6. In a nursery school child get opportunity of playing with other children and also develop other social skills.

UNESCO's Regional Meeting of Experts (1979) argue the early childhood education on the following ground.

1. Increasing concern for social justice and equality in different countries of the world.
2. Early childhood education provide the fulfilment of potential abilities of the children.
3. Over crowding, congestion, and poor living conditions needed for providing better environment to the children.
4. Absence of older people in the family to take care of the children.
5. Custodial and other care of children whose mothers are engaged in economic activities.
6. Need for the provision of nutrition at early stage so as to avoid the consequences of malnutrition.
7. Need for promoting the biological, physical, emotional, social and intellectual growth of the child, and for the ecology in which the child lives.
8. The feeling that it is better to provide early education than to introduce compensatory education activities later.

Scope of Early Childhood Education

The Indian Education Commission (1964-66) has termed the period between 3 and 6 years as the period when pre-school level education can be given to the child. According to this recommendation, the child will join the pre-school between the age of 3 and 4.

Many terms have been used to denote the pre-school education viz., Kindergarten, nursery education, Montesori education and early childhood education. Zakir Hussain Committee on Basic Education pointed out; "The ages three to six may be taken as the normal range for nursery school child" (p. 61, Indore Report).

Whether early childhood programmes also include the primary classes or are limited only to pre-primary programmes appears to vary from country to country from one school system to the other and from one author to the other.

Assumptions

Blank (1970) and Sigel (1973) have provided the following rationale for early 'psycho-educational' experiences to the children:

1. Children are by nature, malleable and their growth and development can be modified extensively in a variety of directions.
2. The earlier one can effect a plausible intervention, the better.
3. The manipulation of early experience will influence psychological functioning.
4. The provision of qualitatively sound experience can modify or compensate for basic lacks in children's environments. Such lacks define the basis on which experiences can be built.
5. Since a well developed cognitive ability is one of man's greater assets, children who fail to fulfil their potential and actualise their capacities are causing both a personal and national loss.

Aims and Objectives of Early Childhood Education at International Level

In England and Wales, social and educational aims with a major emphasis on cognitive development through the medium of language.

In Canada, acquisition of proper health habits, development of language and number concepts, development of moral and spiritual self. Inculcating feelings of adequacy and security and building social values through the medium of play.

France aiming social and educational development of the child through early childhood education. Under social development the areas of emphasis are physical, sensory, aesthetic, manual and social education of the child. Educational development is brought about by recitation, writing, pre-arithmetic and pre-reading activities.

Italy aiming the maximising of the child's real capacities, fostering democratic values, positive self-concept and development of child's personality.

Belgium encouraging physical, intellectual, emotional and social maturation of the child. Development of Language and creative abilities is also emphasised.

Through early childhood education Germany aims building in child's mind the desirable concepts of co-existence, democratic values, social development, independent and creative work.

The Sweden the pre-school goals are broad in scope. They include physical development (body control, manual ability, etc.) social and emotional maturity (habits, adjustment, respect for rules, etc.) and intellectual growth (constructive, creative, language expression, etc.).

In Netherlands early childhood education aiming development of positive and moral and civic values and cultural attitudes. The objective of pre-school education is also to ease transition from pre-school to primary school.

Japan, a developed nation aiming through Kindergarten, which is a pre-school educational institution, at rearing infants in an appropriate environment, thereby helping develop their wholesome mental and physical growth (Austin, 1976).

Aims and Objectives of Early Childhood Education in Asia and Oceania

The countries of Asia and Oceania over emphasising on formal learning and preparatory work for literacy which includes development of reaching, writing and arithmetic skills. The focus of pre-school education should shift from 'education' to 'development'. The development should be multi-dimensional including biological, physical, cognitive, affective and social aspects. In India the Integrated Child Development Services Project (ICDS) started by the Government of India covers the three aspects—the health, nutrition, and education of the pre-school age children. (Report of the Regional Meeting of Experts, UNESCO, 1979).

Aims and Objectives of Pre-School in India According to Education Commission (1964-66)

1. To develop in the child a good physique, adequate muscular coordination and basic motor skills.
2. To develop in the child good health habits and to build up basic skills necessary for personal adjustment, such as dressing, toilet habits, eating, washing, cleaning, etc.
3. To develop social attitudes and manners, to encourage healthy group participation and making the child sensitive to the rights and privileges of being a member of a social group and to encourage him to cooperate, share and take care of property belonging to him as well as others.
4. To develop emotional maturity by guiding the child to express, understand, accept and control his feelings and emotions.
5. To encourage aesthetic appreciation in the child.
6. To stimulate in the child the beginning of intellectual curiosity concerning his immediate environment (awareness of environment), to help him understand the world in which he lives and to foster new interests through opportunities to explore, investigate and experiment.
7. To encourage in the child independence and creativity by providing him with sufficient opportunities for self-expression.
8. To develop in the child the ability to express his thoughts and feelings in fluent, correct and clear speech.

REFERENCES

1. Katz, L. *Early Childhood Education as a Discipline,* Young Children, 1971, 26, 82.

2. Department of Education and Science, Britain, *Low-Cost Day Provision for the Underfives*, 197.
3. Evans, Ellis D. (1975). *Contemporary Influence in Early Childhood Education*, New York: Holt Rinehart and Winston, Inc.
4. Rawat, D.S. (1970) *Pre-Primary Teacher Education Curriculum*. New Delhi: NCERT.
5. MacDonald, James B. *A Proper Curriculum for Young Children*, Phi Delta Kappa 50, No. 7, (March 1969): 406.

3

Great Educators and Early Childhood Education

JEAN JACQUES ROUSSEAU (1712-98)

He was a Swiss by birth. He introduced a movement in education which is called 'Naturalism'. This idea was opposite to the oppressive educational philosophy of Rousseau's days that the children were born 'wicked' and education had to go a long way to socialise them. Rousseau's books *emile* and *social contract* gave his educational philosophy. His ideas and contributions related to Early Childhood Education are:

1. Nature is usually right and training is usually bad.
2. Make games an education and education a game.
3. Teach less from books and more from life.
4. Let the children be free.
5. Harsh discipline and repression is bad.

The importance which Rousseau attached to practical ideas is evident from the quotation, "I do not like explanations in words: young people give them little attention and hardly retain them. Things, objects' I cannot ever repeat often enough that we give too much authority towards with our babbling education that produces only babblers."

JOHANN AMOS COMMONIUS (1592-1670)

He was born in Moravia, Czechoslovakia. Commonius's educational ideas are contained in his famous book *The Great Didactic*. This book gives hints to teachers regarding the aims of education, curriculum, textbooks and methods of teaching.

His ideas and contributions related to early childhood education are:

1. He objected to the frightening method adopted for teaching the students.
2. He believed that punishment was sometimes necessary but should not be associated with school work.
3. Commonius proposed a system of schools covering the period from birth to maturity.

The whole period of growth divided into four distinct grades; infancy, childhood, boyhood and youth. For infancy the school should be the mothers knee. The children should be told 'spiritual' and 'secular' stories. Learning must be take place through the senses. Students shouldn't be over burdened with matters that are unsuitable to their age and comprehension.

4. He pleded for shorter school hours, more play, sounder health, better bodily development and less strain.
5. Children should be encouraged to play games.
6. Teachers should make school work interesting and keep children relaxed.
7. Commonius was strongly in favour of group teaching/ group work.

"He wrote textbooks specially adapted to the needs of children, including the use of pictures to arouse interest and to catch attention.... He put emphasis on the training of senses. This stress has never been lost especially in pre-school work one finds may games, exercises and devices for developing the child's senses of vision, hearing and touch." (Cole, p. 354).

JOHN HENRICH PESTALOZZI (1746-1827)

He was born in Zurich, Switzerland. He was brought up by his mother and a servant. He did not attend school until he was nine years old. Cole Says, "It is not strange that his child under sized and under developed, always indoors, deprived of masculine society, continually dominated by women, and kept from a comprehension of reality out side his home should grow up into a small, weakman, shy and awkward, absent minded, emotional, impressionable. Impractical and intuitive. His character seems to have been formed during these early years of home education" (pp. 459-465).

Pestalozzi ran an orphanage at Burgdort and Munchenbunch and was Founder of a popular school at Yverdon. He wrote a manual for mothers, "How Gertrude Teaches Her Children".

His Ideas and Contributions Summarises as,

1. Education was to be from within not from without.
2. The aims of education was harmonious development of all the powers-moral, intellectual and physical.
3. His method was to put an object before the students and then let them what they saw.
4. He attached great importance to games. His idea was that the child should not remain inactive.

FRIEDRICH WILHELM AUGUST FROEBEL (1782-1852)

He was born in Prussia. He had a difficult childhood full of personal conflicts and financial hardships. He studies pre-school education through his persual of Pestalozzi's *Mothers' Book.* His interest shifted from one job to another. He never felt satisfied and always revolt against something. After eleven years of his teaching, he founded his own school at Keilhan known as the 'Universal German Institute'. He found his Kindergarten at Balnkerburg. He developed play-gifts, packed in boxes with directions for use and illustrated play songs.

His Ideas and contributions are summarised below.

1. The child was the sole source of educational principles, and the teacher simply followed where the students led.
2. The child develops himself through his own creative activities.
3. Self-activity is important for the education of children.
4. Play give joy, freedom, contentment, inner and outer rest, peace with the world.
5. The 'gifts' that made the Kindergarten unique.
6. The use of gifts, he singing of his songs and the playing of various educational games are the key procedures in Kindergarten.
7. 'Play Circle', (Children played games by joining hands in a circle) and 'play song' are the elements of kindergarten.

MARIA MONTESSORI (1870-1952)

Dr. Maria Montessori became interested in the problems of mentally retarded children when she was working toward a medical degree at the University of Rome. After doing Postgraduate work in psychiatry she accepted an appointment as Directoress of Rome's Orthophremic School, an institution for retarded children. She argued that if retarded children could progress to an academic level of normal children one can do much more for the normal children in a properly designed education environment.

Method of Education

Montessori developed materials, mainly of three types: those that are designed to train the senses, those that teach practical skills, and those that help children to adapt themselves to the needs of school life. Montessori's exercises are arranged in series from easy to difficult. For example, on easy exercise consists of cylindrical pieces which are of the same height but different diameters. The children build with blocks such complex figures as: The long Stair, the Broad stair, and the Tower with the help of blocks. This gives training in perceiving length, breadth and thickness.

Her Contributions

Relevance of Montessori system of teacher training for early childhood education, is the child centredness of the method. Concern for learning style development based upon freedom also relevant. A third is the contribution of structure as an assist to this freedom. And a fourth is a commitment to the child's normal development so as to promote "responsible" freedom that is, freedom without license (Benta, 1966).

"She stressed realistic methods of learning through sense experience reminiscent of those of pestalozzi and froebel, but she put more emphasis upon the freedom of the child. In her "houses for children" she infused a spirit of respect for the child and his personality and sought to free him to pursue learning through activities that interested and challenged him. The whole effort of teaching was looked upon as helping the child to learn rather than requiring him to acquire information through formal studies. Her work though suppressed by Mussolini and the Fascist demands for national conformity, influenced schools in Switzerland, Holland,

England and after the second world war, India... If she had been able to systematise her theories through an organised following or in the institutions that prepared teachers they might have been translated, more widely into practice in the schools of Europe" (Butts, 1955, p. 406).

SUSAN ISSACS (1895-1948)

Susan Issacs, who was born in 1865 was a pioneer in the field of child education. She was very keen and perceptive observer. She was greatly influenced by the movement of psychoanalysis. Issacs (1930) says, "My own personal study of young children has served only to increase my deep admiration and gratitude for the genius of Freud in being able to penetrate so deeply and so surely to the actual mind of the little child, through the study of the minds of adults." (p. xi-xii).

Her contributions summarises below:

1. Her books *The Nursery Years* (1927), *Social Development in Young Children*.
2. She illustrates some guiding principles for the every day problems of the children.
3. Her another work *Children and Parent* (1948) dealt with the problems and difficulties of parents and nursery teachers.

She was involved various observational studies as Head of the Department of Child Development at the University of London.

MAHATMA GANDHI (1869-1948)

In 1937, he gave us a sound ideological basis for his scheme of new education called Tai-Talim or Basic Education. At that time he did not think about pre-school education. When he returned from jail in 1944. He had realised the importance of early childhood education. He said, "The real education begins from conception as the mother to up the responsibility of the child. It is very clear that if this new education is to be effective, its foundation must go deeper, it must begin not with the children but with the parents and the community." (Thankaraj, 1968, p. 46).

Essentials of Pre-Basic Education

1. The teacher and parents should cooperate in carrying out the education of young children.

2. The home where the child is born and lives influences him and that becomes the first centre of his education and learning.
3. Pre-school education must not be expensive so that it can reach the millions in the villages.
4. A child has to be active, creative and playful.
5. Though the child in pre-school period cannot be self-sufficient or self-supporting an attempt should be made to develop this quality.

His first experiment in pre-basic education was started in 1945 in the village of Sevagram (Wardha, Maharashtra) under the guidance of Shrimati Shata Narulkar.

Gandhiji's Views on Early Childhood Education

Concept of Education

"That which draws out and stimulates the spiritual, intellectual and physical faculties of the children" (*Harijan*, Sept, 1937). Gandhiji's educational philosophy, according to M.S. Patel, is "naturalistic in setting, idealistic in aims and pragmatic in method" (William Cenker, 1976, p. 105).

Curriculum

Different subjects scheduled as:

Craft	– 3 hours, 20 minutes a day
Music, Drawing and Maths	– 40 minutes
Social studies and Natural Science	– 20 minutes
Physical Training	– 10 minutes

Methods and Approaches

Correlation is the technique to bind education to the child's life and beyond. It is an attempt to combine hand culture with mind culture... Basic education through correlation was directed toward the integration of the student and the integration of curricula (p. 110, William Cenker, 1976).

Role of Teachers

- Teachers role has to be that of a mother.

- One who cannot take the place of a mother cannot be a teacher (*My views on education*, Gandhiji).
- The teachers to cultivate their own effective life and to encounter their students with a "heart-contact" (*Young India*, April, 1929).

JEAN PIAGET (1896-1980)

Implications of Piaget's theories for the nursery and primary school teachers (Beard, 1969) are:

1. They should provide for stories and rhyms and free activity during free periods.
2. The teachers should allow for the development of vocabulary and all kinds of Symbolic representation.
3. The schools may provided with play areas with large toys in which children learn to control their actions and obtain a working knowledge of spatial relationships.
4. The schools may provide a large number of toys and apparatus for construction or for use in imaginative play.
5. Mateiral may be provided for storing, grading and counting by the older and more advanced children.
6. Domestic toys which encourage initiation and playing of roles may also be provided.
7. Water, sand, bricks, drawing materials and paints which gave opportunity for a diversity of construction and representation are also useful.
8. Concept formation and acquisition of skills will become easy if more structured games and activities are provided for the more matural children.
9. When the children are introduced an activity too early the probability is that they will become confused and develop a distaste for learning of this type. Parents should also not encourage early reading but provide more and more activities, exercises without understanding imitation and memory will interfere with concept development.

JEROME S. BRUNER

Bruner, more than Piaget, emphasises the role of environment and education in the individual's development. Bruner says; "Any subject can be taught effectively in some intellectually honest form to any child at any stage of development" (p. 33, *The process of education,* 1960). Children can learn subject matter that can be experienced non-verbally or concretely at much earlier age than many psychologists had assured. According to Klausmeier (1971) many have conveniently ignored this part of Bruner's statement: 'in some intellectually honest form."

Bruner included in his intellectually honest forms, the three modes of his interacting with the environment namely action, imagery, as well as symbols. Bruner's message for the teachers of young children is that they should use all the three modes in their teaching.

LAWRENCE KOHLBERG

According to him all children follow a fixed pattern of moral development, yet all of them do not move to the highest level of moral reasoning. They remain fixed at any one level. The purpose of bringing about moral development, through instruction, is to move the child from one level to the next higher level. The instruction in moral education provides a 'cultural stimulus' to improved moral reasoning. But the cultural stimulus, as environmental force, is insufficient in itself. The children also possess a minimum level of cognitive development for the moral reasoning to grow.

Kohlberg extended Piaget's work and proposed three levels of development:

(i) pre conventional level (pre-moral);
(ii) Conventional level (conventional role conformity); and
(iii) Post-conventional level (self-accepted moral principles); Each of these three levels of development is further subdivided into two stages of moral development.

REFERENCES

1. Banta, T. (1966). *Is these Really a Montessori Method*? Columbus, Ohio: Ohio Psychological Association and Ohio Psychiatric Association.
2. Butts, R. Freeman. (1955). *A Cultural History of Western Education.* New York: McGraw-Hill Book, Co., Inc.
3. Cole, Luella. (1950). *A History of Education-Socrates to Montessori.* New York: Holt Rinehart and Co.
4. *Early Childhood Care and Education* - U.K. Rao.

4

Growth and Developmental Problems During Early Childhood

Arnold Gessel divides the developmental stages into 3 cycles: 1st, 2nd and 3rd and stages A_1, A_2, C, D and A_3. viz.,

	Ist	IInd	IIIrd
A_1	1 ½ -2	5-5½	10-11 stable
B	2-3 yrs	5 ½	11-12 uncontrolable,ego centric
A_2	3-3 ½ yrs	6-7	12-13 yes, sociable
C	3½ - 4	7-8	13-14 introvert
D	4-4 ½	8-9	14-15 extroverts
A_3	4 ½ -5	9-10	15-16 adjustment, stability

The individual repeats the same activity. Three times in the first 16 years. He classified this again into two-period of equilibrium and period of disequilibrium.

Period of equilibrium (A_1, A_2, A_3) and Period of disequilibrium (B, C, D).

Those problems, which the adults cannot handle are called behavioural problems. i.e., deviation from the accepted pattern of behaviour factors.

Factors

1. ***School***

Relationship with the teachers, classmates and with play mates-school.

2. *Family*

Parental attitude – overprotection, rejection, lack of love, broken home, socio economic status, lack of fulfilment of psychological needs, new arrival of siblings, parent's relationship.

Behavioural Problems

- Stealing
- Lying
- Thumb-sucking
- Nail-biting
- Bed-witing (Enuresis)
- Masturbation

I. Masturbation

The cause of masturbation is that over excitation of sex organs, and physiologically.

- Uncomfortable clothing (too fit or tight),
- Due to irritation, due to skin diseases especially in genital organs.

Psychological Reasons

Lack of security, anxiety, frustration, disapproval, scolding, punishment, unkind nature of teachers and parents, all these causes guilty feeling, anxiety, fear. These creates worries in children. This creates behavioural problems in children.

How to be Handle?

Give them comfortable clothings given them "love, affection, security, maintain good relationship with child, avoid civiar punishments, child should be examined thoroughly, avoid words, attitudes and actions, that causes anxiety.

II. Enuresis (Bed witing)

Involuntary passage of urines, usually all the age of above 3 years.

Reasons

(*i*) Physiological anatomical reason, weak bladder, weak kidney (10%-12 month, 30%-18 months, 50%-24 months).

For an average child, bladder control attains at 36 month.

(ii) Nutritional reason – rich in fluid

(iii) General reasons: bad dreams, lack of toilet training, punishment, bathrooms being away from living place, cold winter nights,

(iv) Psychological reasons: maternal overprotection, occurs in mentally retarded children (all enuretics are not mentally retarded), desire for attention (i.e., desire to retain attention shown to them during illness)

Geraad classify enuretic reasons into three.

1. Enuretic response (due to the desire for opposite sex)
2. Regressive response (new arrival of siblings)
3. Revenge response (towards the mother, who is always punishing him)

How it Affects?

1. Refuse to go school
2. Inferiority complex
3. Disturbed sleep
4. Depression
5. Insecurity feeling

How to Handle?

1. Give proper medical care
2. Before going to sleep give less water
3. Give proper toilet training
4. Psychotherapy

III. Thumb Sucking

It is an acquired habit during the 1st year of life.

Causes

1. Fixation due to oral stage
2. It is related to hunger, fatigue, boredom, shame, embarrassment, unpleasant experiences
3. Insufficient lip movements
4. Incompleteness of the sucking phase of feeding

5. Spontaneous withdrawal of the feeding
6. Forced withdrawal
7. Unpleasant feeding situation
8. Feeding schedule (too short feeding time and long interval of feeding)
9. In older children this is due to emotional and intellectual immaturity.

Effect of Thumb Sucking

1. Health problems
2. This leads to cigarette smoking, other oral activities, drinking

How to Handle?

1. Proper feeding
2. Maintain good mother-child relationship
3. Allow them to engage in certain activities.

IV. Nail-biting

Everyday problem of every child-common among with adults and children. Thumb sucking is the expression of satisfaction. But nail biting is the expression of tension.

Causes

Parental punishment, anticipation of difficult task. Thumb sucking people are calm and quiet. Nail biting people are hyper active. Nail biting is a combination of tension and pattern of behaviour of old members. Manicuring-keeping the nails clean and given them pride.

V. Lying

False impression of lying is due to many ways:

1. Imperfection of linguistic tools of children (Calling everybody as dad)
2. Wrong interpretations
3. Insufficient discrimination between a fact and a fantasy
4. Immature illaboration of things, seen and heard

Different Types of Lies

1. Simple reversal of truth (i.e., saying no instead of yes)

2. Exaggerations
3. Fabrications
4. Wrong acquisition

Reasons

1. To avoid punishment
2. Imitate adults
3. Enhancement of self-esteem
4. Desire to seek attention and admiration
5. Monitory

How to Handle?

1. Fear of punishment should be avoided
2. Aware the child about the necessity of telling lie.

VI. Stealing

1. Casual stealing
2. Selective stealing – stealing objects which are required
3. Solitary stealing – stealing by oneself
4. Group stealing
5. Stealing things that are easily accessible - Laraceny

Reasons

1. Loose social and moral
2. Desire for possessions
3. Parent's refusal to buy objects
4. Intellectual inadequacy
5. Intellectual, moral immaturity

How to Handle?

1. Give proper moral training
2. Try to convince the child about their inability

REFERENCES

1. *Textbook on child Development* – Rajammal P., N. Jaya Devadas.
2. *Child Development-Issues, Policies and Programmes* Vol. I, II & III- Dolly Singh.
3. *The Developing Child* – Helen Bee.
4. *Child Development* – Laura E. Berk.

5

Status of Elementary Education in India

Education is the apprenticeship for life.

– Willmott

Every society endeavours to make its citizens educated in the best possible manner. All over the world, education is regarded as a potential investment for the future. An old proverb lays down. "If you are planning for one year, plant rice: if you are planning for five years, plant a tree and if you are planning for the future, educate your children." That is, education is always considered as a ladder of development. It dispels darkness and brings light.

Among various stages of education, primary education has vital role to play. Primary education sets the mould for personality development of the people. J.P. Naik, an eminent educator of our country has very aptly observed "The progress of primary education is an index of the general, social and economic development of the country as a whole." Primary education plays an important role in laying the proper foundation of child's cultural, emotional, intellectual, moral, physical, social and spiritual development. Primary education contributes to national development also. Various studies have clearly demonstrated that countries which have made proper provision for primary education are far ahead with those of inadequate provision.

Elementary education is an all encompassing term which includes the lower primary education. (From class I to V, i.e., 6 to 11 years) and the upper primary education (class VI to VIII, i.e., 11 to 14 years).

Elementary education deserves the highest priority not only on grounds of social justice and democracy, but also for raising the competence of the average works and initialising national productivity. The importance has been well raised by constituent assembly which was responsible for Indian constitution and it is evident from article 45 of the constitution.

The article (45) of the Indian constitution reads "The state shall endeavour to provide, within a period of ten years from the commencement of the constitution for free and compulsory education for all children until they complete the age of 14 years." The 93rd amendment made Early Childhood Care and Education (ECCE) under Article 45.

Concept and Meaning of Universalisation of Elementary Education

Universalisation of elementary education in India means making education available to all children in the age group 6 to 14 years or classes I to VIII standards. Opportunities for this education may be provided through formal or non formal means of education. It signifies that 'education is for all' and not for a selected few. This concept accepts that education is the birth right of every child. This means all children belonging to the rich and the poor, living in town as were as in rural areas and in places which are accessible with difficulty have to be provided with facilities for elementary education.

Universalisation of elementary education means free education. In some of the advanced countries free education means no fees, free books and stationary, free mid-day meals and free school transport. But in developing countries like India, it has not been possible to provide all these facilities free of cost. Of course, if education at this stage is free of tution fee. Other facilities o n a selective basis are also provided.

Important Aspects of Universalisation of Elementary Education (UEE)

1. *Universal Acess*

School facilities should be provided to all the children between the age group 6 to 14 years in the country. The schools be easily accessible within the walking distance of the child. We must provide at least one lower primary 'school within a radius of 1 km and one upper primary school within a radius of 3 km. The ratio of lower primary and upper primary schools must be 3:1.

Eventhough the number of schools have increased we could not provide schools within the walkable distance of students in some rural areas. As per the 6th all India educational survey, there are 8,22,486 schools in the country of which 5,70,455 are primary, 1,62,805 are higher primary. In all these schools, totally there are 17,30,166 primary teachers. There figures indicate the remarkable growth in the number of schools and in the number of teachers in our country. But eventhough we have to improve a lot to attain 100 per cent universal access.

2. *Universal Enrolment*

All children between the age group 6 to 14 years must be enrolled. For this, compulsory legislation must be passed. Under legislation, parents can be fined for not sending their children to schools. However, this provision has remained on paper only.

In the seventies enrolment to class I to V is 74.36 per cent of the estimated population in the age group 6+ to 10+. There percentages vary from 46.99 in Bihar to 116.47 Kerala. The percentage of pupils transferred from standard IV to standard V about 85 per cent. There has been an all round increase in the enrolment of both sexes and now at all levels of education. The student population increased from 2.8 crores in 1950 to 11.4 crores in 1982-83, yielding on growth of 4.5 per cent per annum. Girl's enrolment increased at the compared rate of 55 per cent while comparable rate of boys was 39 per cent per annum. Still the absolute magnitude of girl's enrolment is less. Many factors stand in the way of cent per cent enrolment in std VI. Non availability of upper primary schools in the neighbourhood, inadequate facilities for free education, child labour, reluctance of parents to send girls to mixed schools and so on. The hard core of non enrolled children at the primary stage (class I to V) consists of children from weaker sections of the community like SC, ST, agricultural landless labourers and urban shim dwellers, 2/3rd of the non enrolled children are girls and 3/4th the non-enrolled children are in the none educationally backward states namely, AP, Assam, Bihar, Jammu and Kashmir, Madhya Pradesh, Orissa, Rajasthan, UP and West Bengal.

3. *Universal Participation*

Community participation is the key factor to achieve the universalisation of primary education particularly in multigrade situation. Understanding of child's environment minimises the gap between the school and the community and makes the education need based.

Local community could be defined as a group of people living in a village, panchayat, block, subdivision or district who have common interest and who work together to achieve a common goal, such as achievement of UEE or Education For All (EFA) people living in a neighbourhood may not constitute a community to achieve a common goal unless they are organised 'without organisation it is simply a collection of individuals and cannot function as a unity. In order to function as a viable community, a village level association has to be formed, consisting of a group of persons who can work together and take decision on behalf of the villages.

Community involvement has been considered as a significant input in development of agriculture, health, family planning and employment generating scheme for involving local people for self-help at grass root level and reexamination of assumptions and priorities of planning in many countries. Shift of emphasis is evident from micro level planning to macro level or area level decentralized planning. The purpose is to shift some of the planning task to local community. This movement is increasingly evident in planning universalisation of elementary education.

The rationale of community involvement in UEE can be summed up as,

(i) Due to 'higher social demand for elementary education generated by literacy programme, population explosion and other socio-economic reasons government is funding it extremely difficult to meet the expenditure of UEE. Local support for elementary education has been visualised as a means of supplementing whatever resources the government is in a position to invest.

(ii) The apathy shown by local community towards elementary education could be removed if local community takes interest and support the provision of education.

(iii) Involvement of the community has been visualised as a means to ensure that the school is sensitive to the needs of the community. For example the school curriculum does not focus the local needs and to certain extend alternates the students from life, for example the rural community.

Objectives of Community Involvement in UEE

The involvement of local community in UEE effort has the following objectives:

(i) To involve the people in planning, management and decision making.
(ii) To encourage mobilisation of resources for development of elementary education at local level.
(iii) Sharing of benefits derived from UEE.
(iv) Building social capabilities among all sections of the community in terms of attitudinal change, awareness generation and environment building for UEE.

4. *Teaching-Learning Technologies*

The fundamental principles of teaching-learning technology are:

- Shift from teaching to learning
- Freedom to pace to learn for each child must be provided
- Flexibility in the time-table
- Child's mother tongue should be the medium of initial learning followed by standard language.
- Group activities should be followed by individual activities. Cooperative learning is encouraged in all respect.
- Mature learner can be a good tutor for less mature learner.
- Children learn a lot on their own through learning by errors.
- Teachers is not the only source of wisdom. Teacher is more a facilitator or a intervener.
- Children learn better from their peer group.
- Learning-without fear encourages children in all respects.
- The multi level groupings have widened the scope of child centered activities and is conducive for self-pacing. Their teaching-learning approach is around the principle of learning 'how to learn'. This approach demands the role of teacher as facilitator.

- The holistic approach to teaching was being followed in their schools, which means basically that learning conditions are to be developed/provided according to learners need. Hence maximum scope is to be provided to children for self-pacing.
- Teacher and learner(s) interaction/activities were mainly employed for conceptual learning.
- Interaction between/among the learners were mainly employed for group learning. E.g., Dramatisation, role play, story telling, news reading, group games and exercises. Assembly period is mainly utilised for such exercises.
- Primary children, being concrete stage learners, are exposed to more concrete material which enhances the interaction between/among learner(s) and the material, learning through environment encourages children in all respects.
- The children move according to their own pace of learning, hence not much weightage is given to annual promotion unlike regular schools.
- The schools did not have any head teachers, hence every teacher is his/her own evaluator and monitor. Weekly and monthly meetings of teachers aim to share their success and discuss the difficulties.
- Child centred methodology encourages meaningful activities.

5. *Universal Achievements*

The more enrolment will not guarantee success. Students must learn what they are expected to learn then only UEE becomes successful. But in reality most of the students don't learn even at the maximum level. The important reason are absence of proper motivation from parents and teachers, curriculum is not attractive, defective teaching methodology lack of proper evaluation tool so on, and so forth. All these problems need to be curbed so as to attain our objective of Universalisation Elementary Education.

Growth of Elementary Education During the Post Independence Period

Important Commissions and their Recommendations Regarding UEE

In the educational system evolved by vedic Aryans, a fairly long period of education was prescribed for all children, not on the basis of any state legislation but through more imparative form of a religious practices. Patshalas and Maktabs (The Hindu-Muslim Elementary Schools) catered to the needs of the society with regard to elementary education.

British Period

Education in India under the British Government says Howell was first ignored, the violently and successfully opposed, then concluded on a system now universally admitted to be erranious and finally placed on its present footing.

Gopalakrishna Gokhale made a heroic effort to introduce primary education in the country. But his primary education bill was over thrown by the central registration by an overwhelming majority.

Educational planning in India is mainly based on the recommendations of the education commission under Dr. D.S. Kothari (1964-66). The National Policy of Education adopted by the parliament (1968) was mainly based on this. It stressed free and compulsory education upto the age of 14. The NPE 1986 and its programme of action (POA) shifted the nations emphasis from enrolment to retention. A new scheme called Operation Black Board (OBB) 1987-88 has been evolved in order to retain the child and to make the school environment attractive.

Today, education is a concurrent subject after the constitutional amendments of 1976. The 73rd and 74th, amendments of Indian constitution have strengthened the educational pace through delegation and delimitation of powers to panchayati raj institutions.

Targets and aims of universalisation:

- To be achieved during 6th five year plan.
- All advanced states should achieve at least 10 per cent enrolment for boys in the age group 6-11 and 90 per cent for girls in the same age group.
- All backward states should achieve targets of 100 per cent enrolment for boys in the age group 6-11 special steps may be taken to bring in at least 80 per cent of non-attending children of SC, ST and OBC to schools.

- At least 70 per cent of non-attending children of the rural areas may be enrolled in schools during the 6th plan.

The following special programme to attain targets was recommended:

1. Free distribution of mid-day meal to poor-needy children.
2. Supply of free textbooks and clothing to poor children.
3. Directives may be issued by the centre to the backward states to concentrate on the clearance of the back log of non-attending boys and girls.
4. Setting up of school improvement committees for undertaking intensive drive for bringing non-attending children to schools and also to see to it that enrolled children are retained in schools where school management committees already exist, they may be entrusted with the task.
5. Steps may be taken to enforce attendance, at least to the extent of issuing warning notice and attendance order to the parents of defaulting children.
6. Whenever necessary, the prescribed teacher pupil ratio may be relaxed while sanctioning new schools and additional teachers in backward areas.
7. Provision for part-time schooling may be arranged for these children who are unable to attend regular schools.
8. Identifying special education programmes in backward areas and among socially backward groups of people for educating the parents.
9. Special targets may be fixed for enrolment by the state governments from year to year for each districts greater attention being paid to backward, districts and areas.
10. Separate targets for the enrolment of the children of groups of backward classes may also be fixed at state and district levels.
11. It may be made obligatory for teachers to stay in the vicinity of the school as far as possible. As an incentive, payment of rural accommodation allowance to teachers of rural areas who live within the vicinity of the schools may be considered.
12. Suitable facilities may be given to the children of rural elementary school teachers, studying in high schools.
13. Residential type of schools may be established for children

of teachers working in very backward area and the full cost of education may be done by the government.

Certain crucial educational problems which were examined 3 decades ago, very much remain live issues even now. Our nation faces a variety of problems in its efforts to extricate itself from the influence of an alien educational system which was designed to subserve the interests of a foreign rule and was imposed on a country with a long cultural history.

Education commission (1964-66) states, "The fact what is needed is a revolution in education in turn will set in motion the much desired, social, economic and cultural revolution." Educational reconstruction is crucial and extreme urgent for the national development. It has to be completed will all speed within the lifespan of a single generation.

For a vigorous implementation of recommendations and policies, education should got a much higher priority in the over all development plans. At the same time, the claim for the desired priority can be met to the extend educators are able to convince the nation that education has been successfully revolutionised, that it has been effectively linked with the life, needs and aspirations of the people, that it can help, the country to meet the challenges of hunger, unemployment, ill- health and poverty.

Present Position of UEE

Universalisation of elementary education has been one of the most important goals of education developments in India since independence. Article 45 of the Indian constitution directed states to endevour to provide within a period of 10 years of the commencement of the constitution free and compulsory education to all children up to the age of 14 years. This resolve to be fulfilled by 1960 was, however, severely hampered by several problems, such as the influx of displaced persons after partition and scarcity of resources, both financial and human. As a result, the target rate had to be first revised to 1970, then to 1976, and later to 1990. The target date according to the NPE, 1986 is 1995. The modified policy, 1992 has further revised the target date. It state, "It shall be ensured that free and compulsory education of satisfactory quality is provided to all children upto 14 years of age before we enter the twenty-first century. A national mission will be launched for the achievement of this goal."

Expansion of Elementary Education (Primary and Upper Primary) Number of Institutions (1950-51 and 1998-99)

Table–5.1
Number of Elementary Schools 1950-51 and 1998-99

Category of Schools	*Years*		*Increase*
	1950-51	*1998-99*	
Primary	209671	626737	3 time approx.
Upper Primary Schools	13596	190166	13 time approx.

Table–5.2
Sex wise enrolment at the Elementary Stage 1950-51 and 1998-99

Year	*Primary*			*Upper Primary*		
	Boys	*Girls*	*Total*	*Boys*	*Girls*	*Total*
1950-'51	13.8	5.4	19.2	2.6	0.5	3.1
1998-'99	62.7	48.2	110.2	24.0	16.3	40.3

The total enrolment at the primary stage increased by 5.77 times while for girls the increase in 9 times. At the upper primary stage, the increase is more than 13 times while that of girls the increase is more than 32 times.

Table–5.3
Gross Enrolment Ratios (1950-51 and 1998-99)

Year	*Primary*			*Upper Primary*		
	Boys	*Girls*	*Total*	*Boys*	*Girls*	*Total*
1950-'51	60.6	24.8	42.6	20.6	4.6	12.7
1998-'99	100.86	82.85	92.14	65.27	49.08	57.58

Problems of Universalisation of Education

- Low priority to primary education
- Inequality of educational opportunity
- Low enrolment of the backward sections of the society
- Stagnation
- Wastage

- Low enrolment of girls
- Apathy and poverty of the parents
- Defective curriculum
- Uninspiring methods of teaching
- Lack of suitable reading and writing material for children
- Lack of qualified teachers
- Frequent transfer of teachers
- Lack of effective inspection and academic guidance by the inspecting staff
- Failure to enforce compulsory attendance
- Lack of a suitable admission policy
- Conservative attitude towards co-education
- Inadequate and unattractive school building
- Poor nutrition of children
- Existence of large number of incomplete primary schools
- Lack of part-time facilities
- Group rivalries of local bodies
- Meagre financial outlays
- Overpopulation

Figure 5.1: Rural Habitations/Populations in India Served by Primary and Upper Primary Sections-1993

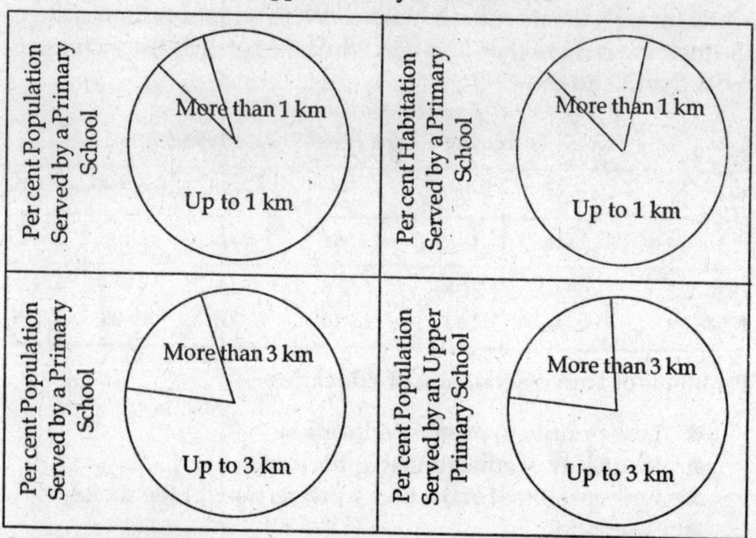

Source: Sixth all India Educational Survey 1993, Vol. 1- Education Facilities in Rural and Urban areas, NCERT.

UEE in India – An Analysis

The last decade of the century definitely marks a significantly positive note in the history of basic education in India. Though the constitution of the country had made a commitment to providing free and compulsory education to all children upto the age of fourteen, the task of providing basic education for all received high priority with concrete plans of action mainly after the national policy on education was launched 1986 and revised in 1992. The educational priorities enunciated by the National Policy on Education (1986) have continued through the nineties. This has been reflected in the higher allocation of resources as well as in terms of clearly defined strategies to achieve the goals of education for all. The world declaration on Education For All (1990) adopted in Jomtien, undoubtedly, gave further fillip to the national commitment for reaching basic education for all children. The Jomtien Declaration together with several positive developments within the country brought to the central stage the need of viewing basic education as a fundamental right of every citizen. India is one of the few countries where during the stabilisation phase of structural adjustment, expenditure on education has been stepped up.

Achievements during the last fifty years are not significant. An estimated 95 per cent of the rural population living in 8,26,000 habitations have a primary school within 1 km and about 85 per cent population have an upper primary school within 3 km. More than 150 million children are currently enrolled covering around 90 per cent of the children in the age group of 6-14 years. Recent surveys on literary rates indicate a phenomenal progress in the nineties. Basic education position and programmes in the recent years have gone beyond the mere emphasis on numbers to focus on quality concerns in basic education, on the education of girls and disadvantaged section of the society, the needs of peoples involvement in basic education programmes and decentralisation of educational management. It is also during this period that World Bank and other international agencies began providing additional funds for speeding up the process of the recent years, it is realised that there are serious problems of gender, regional, sectional and caste disparities in UEE. Despite such significant achievements and positive goal orientation in UEE. A significant proportion of students continue to drop out due to socio-economic and cultural factors as also due to lack of adequate infrastructure, shortage of teachers and nonsatisfactory quality of education provided. The country still is home for more than 800 million illiterates. The challenges have been many. The government is fully seized of the fact that nothing less than a whole hearted national effort both in the public and private sectors would be necessary if India is to emerge as a fully literate and economically vibrant nation of the 21st century.

It is fully recognised that sustainable change and development in basic education is highly conditioned by state specific contexts. Mere funds and schemes from the centre will not guarantee the achievement of UEE goals. It is highly dependent on traditions and values of the local people; commitment and enthusiasm of the state level educational leadership; and capacity to adopt innovative approaches. Viewed from such a perspective authentic accounts of education for all achievement would demand understanding the process, problems and prospects of achieving education for all in every state independently. But, that would have been too ambitious. Indepth analysis of the situation was carried out in four related states, namely Himachal Pradesh, Mizoram, Rajasthan and Tamil Nadu from the EFA process and achievement point of view, the four states get self-related success of Himachal Pradesh come into lime light with the probe study which pointed out how the state has gone way ahead of some of its neighbouring states. The study of Himachal Pradesh captures the factors contributing to the relatively quick progress made by the state. The Mizoram, study brings out the unique role played by local youth and women organisations within the background of pioneering work done by religious organisations. Tamil Nadu case study presents a success story of a different kind. The overt social policies and programmes of the state, including the famous Nutritious Noon Meal Scheme are attributed to have made a significant impact on school enrolment in the 1980s. Subsequently with this apparent success in controlling the population growth, the state has got the opportunity to pursue quality concerns of education for all in an effective manner. Rajasthan cannot stake claim to join the company of the other three states based on quantitative progress in education for all. In the league table of 'States of India, Rajasthan continues to occupy a very low rank. The study regarding this state takes a look at exemplar practices adopted in two major programmes contributing to education for all goals, namely, *Shiksha Karmi* and *Lok Jumbish*.

Table–5.4
Elementary Schools and Teachers, 1982-98

Year	*Schools*	*Teachers*	*Growth Rate Schools*	*Growth Rate Teachers*
		1982-83		
Primary	28290	114713	-	-
Middle	5565	66299	-	-
Total	33855	181012	-	-
		1983-84		
Primary	28543	115705	0.9	0.9
Middle	5635	66399	1.2	0.1
Total	34178	182104	0.9	0.6
		1984-85		
Primary	28847	116305	1.1	0.5
Middle	5691	66849	1.0	0.6
Total	34538	183154	1.1	0.5
		1993-94		
Primary	30329	116396	5.1	0.1
Middle	5593	62192	-1.7	-7.0
Total	35922	178588	4.0	-2.5
		1998-99		
Primary	30844	115697	1.7	-0.6
Middle	5538	61719	-1.0	-0.8
Total	36382	177416	1.3	-0.7

Table–5.5
Drop Out Rate by Class in Tamil Nadu

Year	*Classes 1-5*			*Classes 5-8*		
	Boys	*Girls*	*Total*	*Boys*	*Girls*	*Total*
1990-'91	18.3	22.7	20.3	48.2	49.4	44.5
1994-'95	15.6	17.7	16.5	30.8	39.4	37.7
1998-'99	13.0	16.2	14.5	36.9	33.4	35.2

Table–5.6
Average Number of Teachers Per school; Tamil Nadu, 1990-98

Type of Schools	*'90-'91*	*'91-'92*	*'92-'93*	*'94-'95*	*'95-'96*	*'96-'97*	*'97-'98*	*'98-'99*
Primary	4	4	4	4	4	4	4	4
Middle	12	12	12	11	11	12	12	11

Table–5.7
Schooling Status of Children in Himachal Pradesh

	Boys	*Girls*	*Total*
Currently-enrolled	159	157	316
Never-enrolled	1	4	5
Drop outs	3	5	8
Total	163	166	329

Table–5.8
Growth in Enrolment in Himachal Pradesh Schools

Year	*Primary Stage (Thousands)*		*UP stage (Thousands)*	
	Growth	*Growth rate*	*Growth*	*Growth rate*
1973	420	-	133	-
1978	495	3.34	162	4.02
1986	643	3.32	302	8.10
1993	704	1.30	355	2.30
1997	729	0.87	376	1.46

Table–5.9
Growth in Primary Schools (1986-'99)- Mizoram

Years	*Management*	*Mizoram*	*Percentage of Increase*
1986	Government	813 (79.3)	16.0
	Aided	122 (11.9)	8.0
	Private	90 (8.8)	246.1
	Total	1025 (100)	22.0
1990	Government	900 (81.2)	10.7
	Aided	122 (11.0)	0.0
	Private	81 (7.18)	-3.3
	Total	11.09 (100)	8.19

Years	*Management*	*Mizoram*	*Percentage of Increase*
1999	Government	1043 (82.6)	15.9
	Aided	71 (5.6)	-44.8
	Private	148 (11.7)	70.1
	Total	1262 (100)	8.19

Looking Beyond 2000

Provision of Elementary Education for All Continuing the Unfinished Task

Approaches to achieve the goal of universal elementary education in the years to come have to measure upto the magnitude and complexity of the task which has so far remained incomplete efforts to persue this goal will be guided by three broad concerns.

- The national resolve, as stipulated in the National Policy on Education, to provide free and compulsory education of satisfactory quality to all children upto the age of fourteen years.
- The political commitment to make the right to elementary education a fundamental right and enforcing it through necessary statutory measures.
- Enhantment of 73rd and 74th constitutional amendments which have set the stages for greater decentralisation and a significantly enhanced role for local bodies community organisations as well as voluntary agencies in the efforts towards UEE.

Further, recognising the importance of the primary education sector, the Central Government has been working with the state Government on a 'principle of shared responsibilities for achieving the goals of UEE. This becomes even more important in the context of the commitment to make 'right to elementary education' a fundamental one. With the magnitude of the unfinished task, the government of India will continue supporting the initiatives in primary education which promoting the capacities of the states governments to meet the challenges effectively mobilising additional resources to reach the critical mark of 6 per cent of GDP for education is a goal towards which the country will continue to strive.

Broad-based efforts made during the last fifty years have re-united in a massive expansion of the educational system in the country, raising the overall status of educational provisions in terms of accessibility and participation. The efforts were guided by concerns of equity. Yet, a closer analysis of basic statistics reveal gearing disparities in the progress made, certain sections of population and certain geographical pockets in the country have failed to fully benefit from the investments made in education. Keeping this in view, the approach during the years to come will be specifically deal with the question of equity with focus on the education needs of the following categories:

- Women and girls
- Scheduled castes and scheduled tribe groups
- Working children
- Children with disabilities
- Children from minority groups
- Urban disadvantaged children
- Educationally backward pockets in different states.

REFERENCES

1. *Early Childhood Care and Education* – U.K. Rao.
2. *Principles, Methods and Techniques of Teaching* (2nd ed.) – Aggarwal, J.C.
3. *Primary Schooling in India* – Amarjeet, Sinha.
4. *Primary Education* – U.K. Singh & K.N. Sudarshan.

6

National Curriculum for Elementary Education

Curriculum includes all experiences which are provided to children either inside the school or outside the school, to achieve the objectives of education. Every child gets a number of experiences in the school, some of which are based on the prescribed syllabi and textbooks while some others are based on the co-curricular activities organised by the school.

The process of curriculum development in India lies in between the two extremes of centralisation and decentralisation. It is seen that model exemplars of curriculum are provided by the centre which are utilised by the different boards of education in India. Mudhaliar Commission (1952-53) and the Kothari Commission (1964-66) have provided such points.

The central government formulated the National Policy on Education, 1986, which includes broad guidelines regarding the content and process of education of different stages. Based on this the NCERT has formulated the curriculum framework in 1988.

National Curriculum Framework

The national curriculum framework for elementary and secondary education brought out in 1988, has the following social, cultural, political, economic and pedagogical parameters.

1. All the citizens of the country should enjoy equality of opportunity to pursue education. The curriculum should be an instrument to meet the special needs of disadvantaged sections of the society.

2. To familiarise children with the cultural heritage of country.
3. The citizen must be aware of their duties as also the ideals and principles of the constitution of India to ensure socio-economic and political progress of the country.
4. Promotion of international understanding and peace should also be the objectives of curriculum.
5. In view of the serious problems of population explosion, population related concepts ought to be integrated in the curriculum of different subjects.
6. Other major objectives are the following:

   (a) Preparation of children for future life.
   (b) Total development of child's personality.
   (c) Child centred education.
   (d) Develop creative thinking ability among students.
   (e) Develop scientific temper among children.
   (f) Work should be used as a medium of education.
   (g) Evaluation should be comprehensive and continuous one and made as an integral part of teaching learning process.
   (h) For effective curriculum transaction mass media and educational technology should be utilised.

The national curriculum framework has recommended certain areas of education and their time weightages at the primary and upper primary stages of school education.

Table-6.1
Time Weightage to Various Subjects Schooling

Primary Stage	*Time Allocation*
Mother tongue	30%
Mathematics	15%
Environmental Studies	15%
Health and Physical Education	10%
Arts	10%
Work Experience	20%
Upper Primary Stage	
Three language	32%
Mathematics	12%

(Contd.)

Primary Stage	*Time Allocation*
Upper Primary Stage	
Social Sciences	12%
Science	12%
Health and Physical Education	10%
Arts	10%
Work experience	10%

The proposed curriculum aims at the balanced development of child's personality. The cognitive aspect of personality is taken care of by the curricular areas like language, mathematics, science and social science, while health and physical education and work experience take care of psychomotor aspects. Arts contribute to the development of affective domain of personality.

The National curriculum framework has recommended some core elements which should be taught compulsorily in all parts of the country. These include:

1. History of India freedom struggle
2. Constitutional obligation
3. Content essential for development of national identity
4. Common cultural heritage of India
5. Democracy, secularism, socialism
6. Gender equality
7. Environmental issues
8. Removal of social barriers
9. Small family norms
10. Development of scientific temper

Present Primary Curriculum

Std I & II Integrated curriculum

Std III & IV Mother tongue, English, Maths, Environmental studies, Health and Physical Education, Arts, work experience

Upper Primary Stage

1. Three languages – mother tongue, English, Hindi
2. Mathematics
3. Social Science
4. Health and Physical Education

5. Arts
6. Work experience

Methods of Teaching at Primary Level

Instructional process are the tools of the teacher's trade. Without them there is no teaching. Although all individuals-especially parents-employ various instructional procedures from time to time, it is the school teacher who is expected to master the art of teaching.

The various instructional methods and technique employed at the primary level are the following:

1. Discussion methods, 2. The Dramatic play method, 3. Simulation game method, 4. Inquiry-Discovery method, 5. Project Method, 6. Problem-solving method, 7. Cooperative learning, 8. Peer tutoring procedure 9. Oral reporting techniques, 10. Film and Television Analysis, 11. Teaching through field trips, 12. Using games and kits, 13. Narration, 14. Explicit instruction method (Direct Instruction), Brain storming techniques, Review method, Seminar.

1. *Discussion Methods*

Key Concepts

- Controversial issues provide a sound basis for discussion, accordingly, the intent is not so much the resolution of a problem as it is the weighing of evidence and proposals.
- Open-ended problems (policy problems) are most appropriate for discussion.
- Discussion follows a more-or-less logical sequence of development.

2. *The Dramatic Play Method*

In dramatic play, role playing is used as a vehicle to portray a situation for study and analysis. It involves the spontaneous enactment of a realistic life problem in the realm of interpersonal relationships. When used effectively it may enable learners to improve their responses to a situation, to increase their repertoire of responses and to increase their sensitivity to the feelings of others.

3. *Simulation Game Method*

A simulation is an artificial, condensed representation of reality. It may reproduce the essential details of either a model or an actual situation. Governing the conduct of a simulation are rules that limit or prescribe the actions of players. Rules are incorporated into a game of some type for the purpose of introducing the elements of competition, cooperation and conflict as they normally occur in real life.

4. *Inquiry – Discovery Method*

Like most other instructional approaches, the processes of inquiry are representative of systematised problem solving. This technique is based upon current pupil needs and interests rather than upon organised bodies of subject matter as a starting point. Indeed, the processes of reflective thought are applied by the entire group. The fundamental properties of the inquiry-discovery method are based upon a cooperative experience. This cooperative experience may be teacher-group or teacher individual situations.

5. *Review Method*

Review literally means a re-view or a re-look at something. It is better called a new-view, a view of some problem from a new angle. It is a technique of guiding the pupils in the application of original learning to related situations.

6. *Brain Storming*

Is basically an activity designed to promote creativity. It is a form of discussion which enabled the group to do collective creative thinking. The emphasis in brain storming is on eliciting from the students as many different ideas as possible for more careful consideration at a later time.

7. *Cooperative Learning*

Cooperative structured learning involves more than merely placing children in groups to work together. What distinguishes a co-operative learning group from other groups is that it must function with five elements.

1. Development of Positive Interdependence
2. Teaching of Interpersonal Skills
3. Monitoring
4. Processing and

5. Evaluation in the group work

Cooperative group learning provides for both academic achievement and interpersonal skill development. It unite children with varying backgrounds, ethnic difference and learning styles. Divergent thinking, problem solving and creative tasks can be enhanced through cooperative learning groups.

8. *Peer Tutoring*

The use of one pupil to assist the learning of another child in the same class, must be carefully planned and executed. It is most effective in the realm of mental or motor skills.

9. *Oral Reporting*

The oral reporting technique is basically a means of classifying or expanding information, other supplementary methods must be employed to complete the reflective process.

Importance of Primary Education

The primary stage of education coincides with the childhood years that are the most important years in any person's life. These years lay the foundation for the development of the individual's overall personality. It therefore becomes necessary to provide the child with the right kind of opportunities and experiences in a favourable environment through a good primary education programme. Primary education is a must for every Indian girl and boy in the age range of 5+/ 6+ to 14 years.

Goals of Primary Education

Every child would benefit from primary education in terms of both immediate and long-term gains. In terms of immediate gains primary education must help to develop in the child a feeling of competence to:

- Apply whatever is learnt in school to effectively handle day to day situations.
  Continue further levels of education with confidence in terms of long-term gains it must help the child to acquire those basic knowledge, skills, attitudes and values that will.
- Serve as a foundation for her/his all-round personality and help the child to develop to her/his full potential.

Aims of Primary Curriculum

The primary curriculum aim to achieve the following:

1. To acquire basic skills and processes.
2. To develop critical thinking abilities and problem solving abilities.
3. To enable the child both access and understand relevant information, critically examine it and be able to apply it meaningfully in day to day situation.
4. To prepare the child to live, work and play with others as a member of a group/team/community.
5. To provide children opportunities and experience which help them acquire the capabilities of learning to live together with others in the community.
6. To develop a positive attitude towards labour and to find the importance of dignity of labour.
7. To enable the child to accept values and beliefs different from one's own and treat them democratically.
8. To acquire skill in participating in group activities and develop communication skills to transact in groups.
9. To develop attitude in participating societies and nations political processes.
10. To acquire concepts and abilities for emotional and physical fitness.

Aims of Lower Primary Curriculum

1. The child learns to read and write mother tongue.
2. Various concepts can be assimilated through hearing, reading and observations.
3. The child acquire knowledge of nature, environment, social institutions around him, etc. through his lower primary classes.
4. The child must recognise birds, animals, plants, agriculture, soil, metal, etc. around him.
5. The child observe and study rivers, hills, trees, geographical peculiarities around him.
6. Truthfulness, equality in sex, social manners, cooperativeness dignity of labour, etc. can be acquired at this stage.
7. The child's enquiry capacities, mental power, knowledge skills, etc. should regid during the lower primary stage.

Aims of Upper Primary Curriculum

1. To enable the child to communicate effective in mother tongue, appreciate literature, write fluently in mother tongue. Also able to communicate in English and Hindi.
2. To give practice in observing nature and society.
3. To know natural laws, social and political institution, etc.
4. To give essential awareness about health, hygiene, environmental education, technological discoveries, scientists who affects human history.
5. To give proper attention to personality development at this stage and develop creativity among children.

B. *Different Types of Primary Curriculum*

1. *Child Centered Curriculum*

This is learn-oriented subjects should chosen and taught keeping in view the social, emotional and intellectual needs of children as well as their capabilities and developmental status. Here children construct their own knowledge from their experiences and interactions with the world around them.

2. *Activity-Centered Curriculum*

In activity-centred curriculum subject matter is translated in terms of activities and knowledge is gained as an outcome and product of those activities. Activity is used as the medium for imparting knowledge, attitudes as well as skills.

3. *Integrated Curriculum*

Children at the primary stage are at a developmental level where the learning is meaningful only if the content is prevented in a holistic manner. Their observations and understanding of the things and happenings around are based on totality. Taking this characteristics of children into consideration, ideally the children at primary stage should not be expected to study different subjects in isolation from each other i.e., the total curriculum should be integrated into one whole.

4. *Spiral Curriculum*

The whole curriculum is spread over a number of years. A general treatment of almost all the topics are attempted at the beginning and it is developed in successive years or in the same year at different units according to the mental development of the pupils. In the beginning of the course the whole aspect is given to pupils in a simplified way. Later more and more details of its part are added.

5. *Curriculum Based on Constructivism*

Constructivism emphasises the careful study of the processes by which children create and develop their ideas.

Cognitive Constructivism

According to the constructivist point of view, children literally construct their knowledge of the world and as a result, their level of cognitive functioning. Constructing knowledge and intelligence involves processes of self-directed and self-regulated activity. These processes play major roles in children's assimilation of new information and experiences and accommodation to form new mental schemes. As a result, children continuously structure and restructure experiences in relation to existing schemes of thought. Experiences provide a basis for constructing schemes. Basically stated, "constructivism refers to the fact that knowledge is built by activities children form the inside rather than being transmitted through the senses".

Constructivism has two branches: Cognitive constructivism and social constructivism.

Cognitive Constructivism

Piaget's "Genetic epistemology" and Bruner's Inquiry/Discovery learning are the basis of this theory.

Social Constructivism

Social development theory (L. Vygotsky). The major theme of Vygotsky's theory is that social interaction plays a fundamental role in the development of cognition.

Theoretical Bases of the Present Curriculum

1. *Constructivism (Piaget, Bruner, Vygotsky)*
2. *Multiple Intelligence Theory (Howard Gardner) 1983*

Gardner argued that we do not have one underlying general intelligence, but instead have multiple intelligence each being controlled by an independent system in the brain. Gardner has identified eight intelligence.

1. Linguistic Intelligence
2. Logical Mathematical Intelligence
3. Spatial Intelligence
4. Bodily-Kinesthetic-Intelligence
5. Musical Intelligence
6. Interpersonal Intelligence
7. Intrapersonal Intelligence
8. Naturalistic Intelligence

According to Gardner each person has unique profile of these intelligences, with strengths in some areas and weakness in other.

3. *Emotional Intelligence (Dr. Daniel Goleman -1995)*

Emotional Intelligence is a unitary ability (related to, but independent of standard intelligence) helpful in knowing, feeling and judging emotions a close cooperation with one's thinking process to behave in a proper way, for the ultimate realise of the happiness and welfare of the self in tune with others.

Constructivism in Primary Education

1. Emphasises learning rather than instruction.
2. Learning considered as a process.
3. Priority to 'how to learn' than 'what to learn'.
4. Nurtures the learners instinctive curiosity
5. Encourages the spirit of inquiry
6. Accepts the role of exploring and experiences in learning
7. Mental models of learners taken into consideration
8. Support cooperative learning
9. Encourage dialogue and communication among pupils and teachers
10. Encourage learning through life situations.
11. Strong foundation of cognitive theories
12. Performance is given importance in evaluation
13. Teacher as a facilitator, co-learner, diagnostician, democratic leader, continuous learners, planner, researcher, organiser, evaluator, produces, social connecter, and collector.

Salient Features of Present Primary Curriculum

1. Learner centred-activity oriented
2. Individualised learning – multiple learning
3. Importance given to process and product of learning
4. Continuous and comprehensive evaluation
5. Cooperative learning as a major strategy
6. Grading in evaluation
7. Strategies like projects, seminars, debates, field trips, assignments, club activities, etc. are usual for to transact curricular objectives effectively.
8. Integrated approach
9. Spiral approach
10. Wake up activities
11. More importance to activity
12. Importance of fantancy
13. Importance give to home learning environment

General Objectives of School Curriculum

School curriculum, on the whole, should aim at enabling the learners to acquire knowledge, develop concepts an incalculate skills, attitudes, values and habits conductive to the all-round development of their personality and commensurate with the social, cultural, economic and environmental realities at national level.

School curriculum should, therefore, help to promote development in learner of:

1. Language abilities and communication skills needed for social living and further learning.
2. Competencies that facilitate mathematical operations and their applications in day-to-day life.
3. Knowledge, attitudes and habits necessary for keeping physically fit and strong in conformity with normal developmental pattern.
4. Qualities that make a man socially effective and happy in various social settings, such as friendliness, co-operativeness, compassion, self-discipline, self-criticism, self-control, humour, courage, commitment, to social justice and equality of sexes.

Figure. 6.1: A diagrammatic presentation of the sequential steps in a strategy for effective curriculum transaction (Cognitive learning)

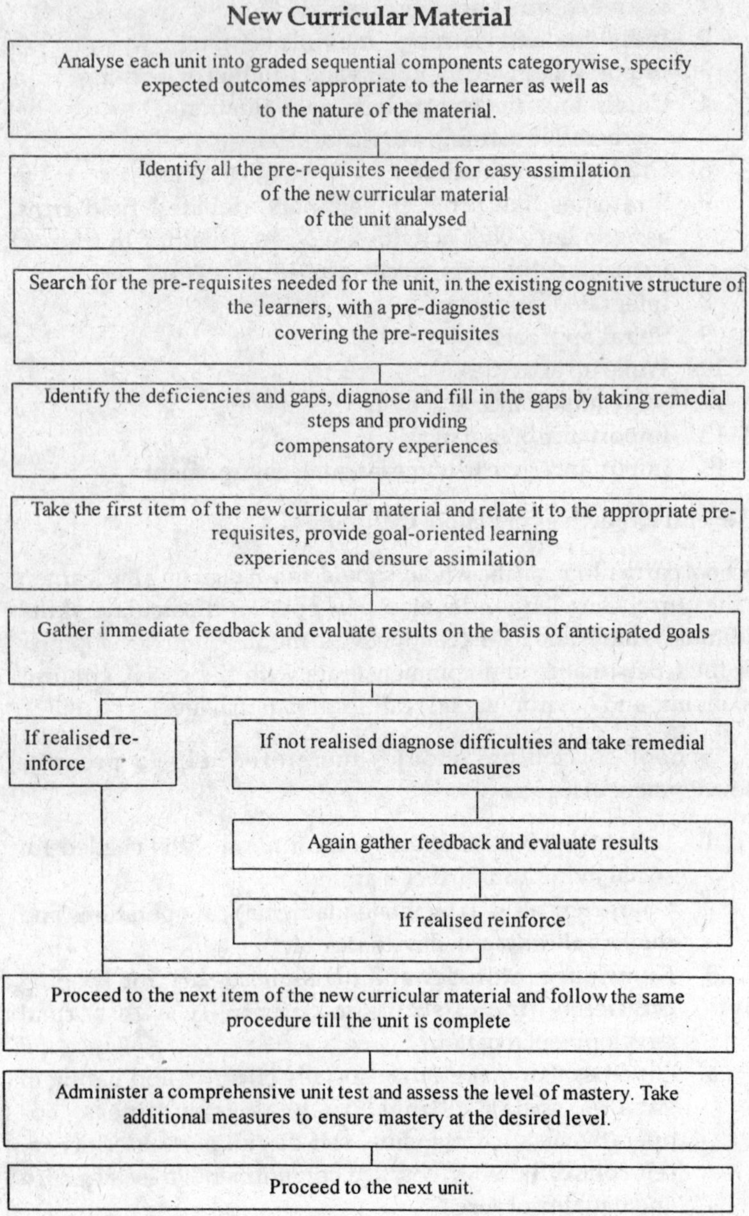

5. Moral and character values such as honesty, truthfulness, dependability, courtesy, fearlessness, compassion, etc.
6. Pre-vocational/vocational skills, willingness to work hard, entrepreneurship and dignity of manual work necessary for increases productivity and job satisfaction.
7. Ability to appreciate and discover beauty in various life situations and integrate it with understanding of the environment and its limited resources and the need of conservation of natural resources and energy.
8. Appreciation of various consequences of large families and over population and need of checking population growth.
9. Understanding of the diverse cultural and social systems of people living in different parts of the country and the country's composite cultural heritage.
10. Knowledge of scientific methods of enquiry and its use in solving problems, along with scientific temper characterised by spirit of enquiry, courage to question and objectivity leading to elimination of obscurantism, superstition and fatalism.
11. Divergent and independent thinking necessary for self-learning and for lifelong learning leading to creation of a learning society.

Emerging Role of Teacher

The recent research in school and teacher effectiveness has indicated that the role of a classroom teacher at primary stage has been changing with times. Today, the effective teacher is considered to be one who has a repertoire of diverse organisational strategies and teaching techniques, grounded in clearly articulated goals and secure knowledge of subject-matter and pupil learning, who then selects from this pedagogical repertoire according to the unique practical needs and circumstances of his or her professional situation rather than the dictates of educational fashion, ideology or habit. On this basis, the notion of 'good' of 'effective' practice as a specific or singular set of processes is replaced by the pluralism of 'good practices' and the thrust of discourse now is to improve upon the 1970s/1980s preoccupation with prescribing the exact form of such practices with a sharper delineation of the principles which might underpin them, whatever form they take.

REFERENCES

1. Government of India, *National Policy on Education*, MHRD, New Delhi, 1986.
2. Government of India Programme of Action, MHRD, New Delhi 1992.
3. Government of India Education Commission (1964-66). New Delhi.
4. Govt. of India, *Education and National Development the Report of Education Commission*, New Delhi: Manager of Publications, 1966. pp. 149-151.
5. *Primary Schooling in India* – Amarjeet, Sinha.

7

Constitutional Provisions Related to Elementary Education

Introduction

The Indian constitution is the bulkiest written constitution in the world. Our constitution which came into existence on 26th January 1950 consists of 444 articles including subclauses (originally it has 395 articles) and 24 parts and 12 schedules. As education is an integral part of any country our constitution also provides some provisions to Education. Recently the parliament approved the bill that education as one of the fundamental right, earlier it was in the state list. From 18th December 1976 by the 42nd amendment of the constitution education came under concurrent list.

Constitutional Provisions for Education

The following are the important articles that related to education.

Article 21 (A): Article 21(A) states the fundamental rights of Indian citizens. The new Article 21(A) says "the state shall provide free and compulsory education to all children of the age six to fourteen years in such a manner as the state may, by law, determine".

Article 51 (A): defines the fundamental duties of the citizens. The new clause to Article 51A(K) states that "It shall be the duty of every citizen of India who is parent of guardian to provide opportunities for education to his child or as the case may be, ward between the age of six and fourteen years."

Article 25: "No religious instruction is given in any educational institution".

Article 28(i): "No religious instruction shall be provided by any educational institution wholly maintained out of states fund."

Article 28 (ii): "Nothing in clause (1) shall be applied to an educational institution which is administered by the state but has been established under any endowment (OR) trust which requires that religious instruction shall be imparted in that institute."

Article 28 (iii): "No person attending any educational institution recognised by the state (OR) receiving out of the state fund shall be required to take part in any religious instruction that may be imparted in such institutions (OR) attend any religious worship that may be conducted in such institution (OR) in any premises attached there to unless such person (OR) if such person is a minor his guardian has given his consent there to."

Article 29 (i): "It provides that any section of citizens residing in the territory of India (OR) any part there of have the freedom to preserve the script (OR) follow any language (OR) culture of its own shall have the right to conserve the same."

Article 29 (ii): "No citizen shall be denied admission into any educational institution by the state (OR) receiving aid out of the state funds on grounds only of religion, caste, race, language (OR) any one of them."

Article 30: "It states that the state shall not in granting aid to educational institution discriminate against any educational institutions on the grounds that it is under the management of a minority whether based on religion (OR) language."

Article 30(i): "All minorities whether based on religion (OR) language shall have the right to establish and administer educational institution of their choice."

Article 30 (ii): "The state shall not discriminate against any educational institution in respect of granting aid on the ground that it is under the management of minority whether based on religion (OR) language."

Article 26 (i): "Any section of the citizens residing in the territory of India (OR) any part their of having a distinct language, script (OR) culture of its own shall have the right to converse the same."

Article 25 (i): "Indian constitution guarantees all the citizens the right to have freedom of conscience and right to profess, practice and propagate any religion."

Article 46: "The state shall promote with special care the education and economic interest of the weaker sections of the people and in particular of the SC/ST & Shall protect them from social injustice and from all forms of exploitations."

Article 350 (A): "It shall be the endeavour (attempt) of every state and every local authority to provide adequate facilities for instruction in the mother tongue at the primary state of education belonging linguistic minority group."

Education as a Concurrent Subject

The forty-second Amendment 1976 brought about drastic changes in the Indian Constitution. It put education, hitherto a state subject on the concurrent list. The Swaran Singh Committee said 'Agriculture and education are subjects of prime importance to the country's rapid progress towards achieving desired socio-economic objectives. This amendment makes central and state government equal partners in framing educational policies. Union becomes supreme over states in enacting law regarding education. The executive power is given to the union to give direction to the states. The states have powers limited to the extent that there do not impede (OR) prejudice the exercise of the executive powers of the union. The centre can implement directly any policy decision in any state, national institutes like UGC, NCERT and National bodies like CABE have high power and strength to shape the education of the country in all the states.

Universalisation of Elementary Education

Indian had a glorious past: once upon a time cities like Mohanjo Daro and Harappa and ports like Lothal flourished here. Famous physicians and surgeons like Charaka, Sushrutha and Vagabhata lived in this country. Mathematics and astronomy have got important place. From the four conrners of the world scholars came to use to Nalanda and Taxila in search of humanity.

Gone are those days. Today we are the most illiterate nation in the world, the most sick nation in the world, the most hungry nation in the world. Even the very freedom for which our forefathers faught in danger.

We wrote in our constitution (Article 45) that "The state shall endeavour to provide within a period of ten years from the commencement of the constitution for free and compulsory education for all children until they complete the age of 14 years."

Sixty years ago Mahatma Gandhi said "We have the education of this future state. I say without fear of my figures being challenged successfully, that today India is more illiterate than it was fifty (OR) hundred years ago, and so is Burma, because the British administrators when they came to India, instead of taking hold of things as they were, began to root them out.

Status and Achievement of UEE in India

There is no gain saying in stating the fact that a large majority of these million of illiterate and non-enrolled and/or out of school children are residing in South Asia. That is a majority of this population is in India is not only the most embrassing but also the most disturbing aspect of the efforts we have made so far towards achieving the cherished goal of universalisation of elementary education. That is not all the unfortunate part of the story is that the country is now here near achieving even the goals of universalisation of primary education. The earlier this stark reality is recognised by one and all in India, the better it will be for all of us – the macro level high profile administrator and the low profile micro level field workers. Resolutions (OR) promulgations of ordinances as well as public clichés are just not going to make an iota in the existing situation. i.e., being almost at the bottom of the list of countries in providing basic education for all.

All available information strongly indicates that the time of attainment of independence in 1947, the health and education scenario in the country was, to say the least, dismal, if not altogether hopeless young children and mothers were an utterly neglected lot. The mortality rate was very high and morbidity rampant in the young population due to talk of proper health care and adequate nutrition. The level of achievement in elementary education was extremely low in almost all respects. Thousands of villages and rural habitations, particularly those in hilly and mountainous regions, were without schools. only one child out of three in the age group 6-11 and one child out of eleven in the age group of 11-14 were enrolled in schools. Educational inequalities were large, especially between one region and another between urban is rural areas between boys and girls and between the advanced and intermediate castes, on the one hand and SC/ST and OBC on the other. The quality of elementary education was poor and the rates of drop-out and stagnation were extremely high.

India undertook the gigantic task of national construction aimed at bringing about socio-economic transformation and at creating a new social order based on the principles of democracy, social-justice and secularism. That without providing education to masses, it was well high impossible to achieve economic development and to establish a just and egalitarian society, came to be accepted as an indisputable fact by those who frame the Indian constitution. Hence the total commitment to making the provision of free and compulsory education for all children in the age group 6-14. This cherished goal should have been attained by the year 1960. However, this target date had to be first revised to 1970 then to 1976 and later to 1988. The new target date according to the resolution in the National Policy on Education 1986. One would wish that as a nation we should have been more discreet in fixing the target which were realistic and within our reach.

73rd and 74th Constitutional Amendments and their Implications for Elementary Education

Though the Panchayati Raj Institutions have been in existence for a long time, it has been observed that these institutions have not been able to acquire the status and dignity of variable and responsible people's bodies due to a number of reasons including absence of regular elections, prolonged supersessions, in sufficient representation of weaker sections like SC/ST and women, inadequate devolution of powers and lack of financial resources.

Article 40 of the constitution, which enshrines one of the directive principle of state policy lays down that the state shall take steps to organise village panchayats and rest them with such powers and authority as may as necessary to enable them to function as units of self-government. In the light of the experience of the last 50 years and in view of the shortcomings, which have been observed it is considered that there is an imperative need to enshrine in the constitution certain basic and essential features of Panchayat Raj institutions to impart certainly, continuity and strength to them.

A Gram Sabha is empowered to exercise such powers and perform such functions at village level as the legislature of a state may by law provide Article 243A.

Article 243B provides for the constitution of Panchayats at the village, intermediate and district levels. However Panchayats at the intermediate level may not be constituted in a state where population does not exceed twenty lakhs.

Legislature of a state is empowered to make provisions with regard to composition of panchayats provided that the ratio between the population of the territorial area of the panchayat at any level and the member of seats in such panchayat to be filled by election shall be same throughout the state.

The chairperson of a panchayat at the village level shall be elected in such manner as the legislative of a state may by law, provide and a panchayat at the intermediate level (OR) district level shall be elected by and from amongst, the elected members thereof 243D provides for reservation of seats and offices of chairpersons to the SC/ST and women and women belonging to the SC/ST.

The duration of every panchayat shall be five years (Article 243E) 243 F provides for disqualification for being chosen as and for being a member of Parliament if he is disqualified to contest the elections to the legislature of the state concerned. Provided no person shall be qualified to contest the election if he is less than twenty five years of age if he has attained the age of twenty one years.

The provisions of the newly inserted part IX of the constitution (73rd Amendment) Act 1993 shall apply to the Union Territories provides that the president is empowered to direct that the provisions of this part shall apply to any Union Territory (OR) part there of subject to the subject exceptions and modifications as he may specify in the notification.

In many states local bodies have become weak and ineffective on account of a variety of reasons, including the failure to hold regular elections, prolonged suppressions and inadequate devolution of powers and functions. As a result, urban and local bodies are not able to perform effectively as vibrant democratic units of self-government.

Having regard to these inadequacies, it was considered necessary that provisions relating to urban local bodies are incorporated in the constitution particularly, for:

(i) Putting on a firmer footing the relationship between the state government and the urban local bodies with respect to
  (a) the functions and taxation powers and
  (b) arrangements for revenue sharing

(ii) ensuring regular conduct of election

(iii) ensuring timely elections in the case of supersessions

(iv) providing adequate representation for the weaker sections and SC/ST and women.

Accordingly, it has been proposed to add a new part relating to the urban local bodies in the constitution to provide for

(a) the constitution of three types of municipalities.

(b) composition of municipalities, which will be decided by the legislature of state

i. Representation of chairperson of committees, if any at ward (OR) other levels in the municipalities.

(c) Election of chairperson of a municipality in the manner specified in the state of law.

(d) Constitution of committees at ward level (OR) other level (OR) levels within the territorial area of a municipality as may be provided in the state of law.

(e) Reservation of seats in every municipality:

  (i) for SC/ST in proposition to their population of which not less than one-third shall be for women.
  (ii) For women which shall not be less than one-third of the total number of seats.
  (iii) In favour of backward class of citizens if so provided by the legislature of the state.
  (iv) For SC/ST and women in office of chairpersons as may be specified in the state of law.

(f) fixed tenure of 5 years for the municipality and re-election within a period of six months of its dissolution.

(g) Devolution by the state legislature of powers and responsibilities upon the municipalities with respect to preparation of plans for economic development and social justice and for the implementations of development schemes as may be required to enable them to function as institutions of self-government.

(h) Levy of taxes and duties by municipalities assigning of such taxes and duties to municipalities by state governments and for making grants in aid by the state to the municipalities as may be provided in the state law.

(i) A finance commission to review the finances of the municipalities and to recommend principles for
   - (i) determining the taxes which may be assigned to the municipalities.
   - (ii) sharing of taxes between the state and municipalities
   - (iii) grants-in-aid to the municipalities from the consolidated fund of the state.

(j) audit of accounts of the municipal corporations by the comptroller and Auditor General of India and laying of reports before the legislature of the state and the municipal corporation concerned.

(k) making of law by a state legislature with respect to elections to the municipalities to be conducted under the superintendence, direction and control of the chief election officer of the state.

(l) application of the provisions of the Bill to any Union Territory (OR) part thereof with such modifications as may be specified by the president.

(m) Disqualifications for membership of a municipality.

(n) Bar of jurisdiction of courts in matters relating to elections to the municipalities.

Directive Principles in Article 45

Free and Compulsory Primary Education

Article 45, under directive principles of state policy lays down. "The state shall endeavour to provide within a period of ten years from the commencement of this constitution, for free and compulsory education for all children until they complete the age of fourteen years." Now Article 45 also dealt with Early Childhood Care and Education (ECCE).

NATIONAL AND STATE POLICIES ON ELEMENTARY EDUCATION

National System of Education

The New Education policy has been designed to see that a national system of education is created and all imbalances and disparities are removed in all sectors of education. The national system is based on a national curriculum framework which contains a common core along with other components that are flexible. The common core includes the history of Indian's freedom movement, our constitutional obligations, our cultural value system, national heritage, inculcation of scientific temper, observance of small family norms, secularism, democracy and socialism. The National system of education envisages a common educational structure of 10+2+3 which has been already accepted in all part of the country.

National Literacy Mission

To promote equality it will be necessary to provide for equal opportunity to all not only in access, but also in the condition for success. Adequate provisions have been made in the policy for education of SC/ST minorities. Handicapped and other educationally backward sections and areas.

Highest Priority

The New Education Policy, however gives the highest priority to solving the problems of children dropping out school and will adopt an array of meticulously formulated strategies based on micro planning, and applied at the grass roots level all over the country, to ensure children's retention at school.

Operation Blackboard

It is the endeavour in the New Education Policy to provide minimum essential facilities in primary, schools viz., two reasonably large rooms that can be used in all weathers, the necessary toys, equipment, maps, charts, other learning material including the blackboard. An 'Operation Blackboard is being undertaken throughout the country as a part of the school improvement programme. It symbolises doing things at the right time, the right sprit and the right way by the right people. It is a programme of providing minimum essential facilities to all the primary schools in the country.

Women's Education

Education will be used as an agent of basic change in the status of women and women's empowerment. A component of women's development is being added to all the on-going programmes of the Department. For example,

(a) Stress on women teachers, while providing an additional teachers under operation blackboard.
(b) Non-formal Education to be treated as a programme of courses and special training of women instructors.
(c) National Literacy Mission to have a special focus on women's equality and running of centres for women.
(d) In vocationalisation, programmes for women's vocationalisation have been given special stress.
(e) A large programme of women's polytechnic, i.e. being taken up in technical education.
(f) Women's studies would continue to receive attention in higher education.

Navodaya Schools

The New Education policy fully takes care of providing open avenues of quality education to the masses. This was the concept behind the proposal to establish model schools now called Navodaya schools in every districts in the country. These schools are meant for the talented children of poor living in rural, tribal and hilly areas. The major thrust of these Navodaya Vidyalaya's is to promote national integration by taking the children from one part of the country to another and put them together so that they grow up another as Indians breaking the traditional, social, regional and economic barriers. On the contrary, the new vidyalayas will be pace setting institution with full scope for innovation and experimentation which will cater to the creative expression and ability of the rural poor children.

Vocationalisation

Vocationalisation has received a very high priority in the new policy. It is envisaged that the point council of vocational education will be an umbrella body under the ministry of Human Resource Development which will also incorporate representation from all existing vocational education/training authorities and state government.

Open University

The New Education policy also provides for rural university which will be developed on the lines of Mahatma Gandhi's revolutionary ideas on education for the transformation of rural areas.

The first open university in India was established on 20th August, 1982 at Hyderabad and was inaugurated by the president of India. The open university is a direct outcome of the failure of the formal system of education to deliver the goods.

Examination Reforms

The New Education policy lays special emphasis on evaluation process and examination reforms. It lays down that assessment of performance is an integral part of any process of learning and teaching. As part of second educational strategy examination should be employed to bring about qualitative improvement in education.

National Policy of Education 1986

The National Policy of Education 1986 marks a significant step in the history of education in free India. It was initiated by the Government of India to enable the country to promote its socio-cultural identity and to equip the country to face the challenges of the twenty first century. In 1985, the Government published "The Challenge in Education" an important document containing guidelines for the future policy of education in India. After detailed debates and discussions at various levels, the national policy of education was formulated and it was passed by the Parliament in 1986.

The national policy of education is formulated on the basis of the directive principles and values enshrined in the constitution of India. The cultural and spiritual tradition of India, democratisation, national integration and modernisation are seriously discussed in this policy.

The National system of education, Navodaya Schools, Vocational targets, de-linking degrees from jobs, performances and accountability, Indian educational service, etc. are some of the admirable innovations in the new education policy.

Tangible results have been obtained in Operation, Black Board, Navodaya schools, mass-orientation of teachers and computer training and literacy mission.

REFERENCES

1. *Constitution of India* – by C.K. Jain.
2. *Constitution Amendment in India* – by Dr. R.C. Bhardwaj.
3. *School Education in 1990's* – NCERT Publication.
4. *Teacher and Education in Indian Society* – by Dr. K.V. Eapen.

8

Training Methods in Early Childhood and Elementary Level

ROLE PLAY

Role play is acting out an incident/situation by understanding the dynamics of the role. No script of dialogues are provided to the characters.

Types of Role Plays

1. *Small unit role playing:* The trainee group is divided into smaller groups consisting of 4-5 trainees. Each group separately role plays the same situation and prepares report on their presentation.
2. *Sequential Role Playing:* Different people present a role play on the same situation.
3. *Role Reversal:* Role playing of a situation where two individuals are involved. After presentation of role play the roles are reversed.

Advantages and Uses

1. It makes possible to bring the field situation in the class.
2. It increases group interaction.
3. Helps the trainees to understand others viewpoints.
4. Holds interests of the trainees.
5. Roles and responsibilities of others are better understood.
6. Provides opportunity to the trainees to know their own capacity in dealing with problems related to human relations by developing skills in problems diagnosis and solving.

Disadvantages

1. Role play consumes a lot of time
2. Unless summarised to focus attention on learning outcomes from the role play, it loses its meaning.

Demonstration

Demonstration is teaching by doing. This method is used when the trainer wants to explain a process or method of operation and when no amount of detailed explanation would help learning. This method is useful when a skills is to be taught to the trainees.

Advantages

1. It is useful in teaching manual skills.
2. It teaches teamwork and enhances dignity of labour.
3. It generates and sustain interest and attention.
4. It makes understanding of the complex ideas easier on the part of students.
5. It fosters spirit of confidence among students and makes learning alive.

Disadvantages

1. It requires special arrangements.
2. Demonstration may be sometimes costly investment of time money and other resources.

Case Study Method

Case study is a verbal/visual presentation of a problem or a situation that is experienced in a workplace. To use a case study in a training situation, it is discussed by trainers in groups. The aims of case study method is to develop among the trainees ability to locate problems, analyse causes and suggest alternative solutions to a given situation or problem.

Advantages

1. There are several ways of dealing with a problem.
2. It is essential to analyse each line of action before the final decision is taken.

Limitations

1. Trainees should have the knowledge and experience to solve the case problem .
2. Learning from this method depends to a large extend on the performance, knowledge, experience and participation of the trainees.

Field Visits/Observational Visits

Field visits, or observational visits is another useful training method when trainees are taken for a day or two, to observe the actual functioning of an institutional programme. Supplementing classroom teaching with field visits/observational visit, provides a frame of reference to classroom teaching gives trainees first hand observation of objectives and functioning of different types of agencies that are not transportable or reproducible in the classroom.

Advantages

1. This helps the trainees to gather authentic information and new ideas that can be used later.
2. Interest level remains high as it relates theory to practice.
3. The understanding of trainees is enhanced as the trainees gain proper perspective.

Disadvantages

1. It becomes expensive in terms of time and money.
2. It requires a lot of preparation before hand.

Lecture Method

Lecture method is the most popular training method, since, it gives a trainer the scope to cover a wide range of subject matter in a limited time. Lecturing is a still which can be mastered through practice. To use lecture method successfully, the trainer must organise the session well. The trainer should follow the step viz.,

(a) Acquire the necessary knowledge on the topic taught
(b) Planning the session
(i) Introduction of the topic
(ii) Stating the objective, purpose of the topic
(iii) Linking the topic to the knowledge previously acquired by the trainers

Advantages

1. Useful for providing basic information that the trainees need to know as also to review, clarify, emphasise and summarise certain topics and concepts.
2. Gives the trainer scope to cover the subject matter in a limited time and in a predetermined sequence.
3. Convenient method for the trainees to take down notes.
4. Can be easily combined with any other method of training.

Limitations

1. Permits little exchange of idea unless combined with exercises, group discussions, question answers, etc.
2. Inappropriate for teaching skills.
3. Requires a skilled trainer; otherwise the lecture may become dull and the trainees remain passive listeners.

To overcome the limitations mentioned above, the following suggestions are considered.

1. Pose questions to the trainees in between the lecture.
2. Illustrate the topic through examples/experiences
3. Use A.V. aids such as blackboard, slides, charts, posters, flannel graphs, transparencies, etc.
4. Use lecture method in combination with some other training method such as buzz, brainstroming, etc.

Buzz Method

"Buzz" method gets its name from the buzzing sound that is generated when 5-6 groups simultaneously discuss an issue. Buzz method may be used in combination with lecture method. This method may be used to seek the participation of the trainees for consolidation of points or the area under discussion, which would otherwise stated by the trainer himself. The outcome of discussions is generation of ideas and views not necessarily a consensus.

To Use the Buzz Method

1. The trainer gives an introduction of the topic to be covered.
2. The group more than 20 participants is divided into smaller groups. Buzz groups are formed when a sub-topic of the lecture requires exchange of ideas/views.

3. Trainer briefs the trainees on the discussion which have to take place in the buzz groups and announces the time limit of 5-6 minutes. Trainer must state issues/problem to be discussed very clearly.
4. At the end of the given time, a representative from each group presents the suggestions/solutions of the group.
5. Trainer notes down the suggestions on the blackboard and then begins lecture based on these ideas.

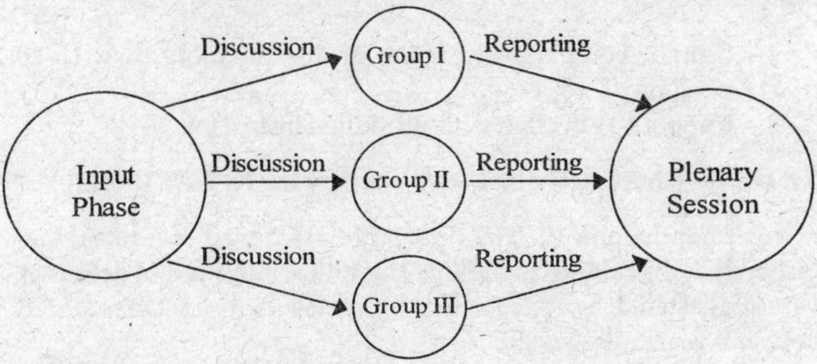

Figure 8.1: Buzz Session

Advantages

1. It can draw all the participants including reluctant ones.
2. There is a good exchange of ideas and pools suggestions.
3. It helps the trainer to get a quick feedback.

Disadvantages

1. Time for discussion is not enough, thus there can be usually no consensus.
2. In short time, group may not be able to organise itself.

Brainstorming Method

Brainstorming involves storming the brains of the trainees with a statement or a problem, so as to get their spontaneous reactions. No suggestions or idea is taken as incorrect, when the trainees are responding. In this way large number of ideas are generated as also the trainer gets to know the level of understanding of the trainees on a particular subject. Brainstorming method can be used effectively in combination with lecture method.

Uses

1. Stimulates trainees participation
2. Develops creative solutions to problems

Advantages

1. Its fast moving face adds interest
2. Valuable ideas emerge though just 50 per cent of these are usable.

Limitations

1. Cannot be effectively if the group has more than 15-20 persons.
2. Cannot be effective without skilled instructor.

List of Pre-School Activities Suggested by the NCERT (India)

In workshop help in 1970 by the National Council of Educational Research and Training (NCERT), the following types of activities were suggested. It can be seen that for each activity a set of required materials is also suggested.

1. Play Activities

Activities	*Materials*
1. Pushing, jumping, throwing, paddling, crawling, sliding, swinging, etc.	Wheel cuts, balls, tricycles, wooden boxes, slides, swings, see-saw, merry-go-rounds, rotating platforms, etc.
2. Walking, hopping, skipping	Skipping ropes
3. Sand play	Sand tray, and sand box toys, etc.
4. Constructional play	Building stocks, etc.
5. Doll's house play	Doll's loud material
6. Clay or plasticine modeling	Clay, dough or plasticine
7. Drawing	Chalk-board, chalks, papers and pencils
8. Bead stringing	Bead and string.
9. Water play	Tub for water and floating toys.
10. Hammering	Hammer, nails, pieces of wood.
11. Imaginative play	Odds and ends for imaginative play
12. Interpreting pictures	Picture-books and scrap-books
13. Gardening	Tools for digging earth, trimming plants, etc.

2. Practical Life Activities

Activities	*Materials*
1. Cleaning teeth, hands, face and other body-parts	Soap, water, brush, paste, towel, basin tongue cleaner.
2. Dressing/undressing	Sets of dresses
3. Buttoning and lacing	Buttoning and lacing frame
4. Combing hair	A comb
5. Using a handkerchief and washing it	Handkerchiefs and washing soap
6. Cleaning and polishing shoes	Polish, selve and piece of cloth
7. Opening and closing doors and boxes	Boxes
8. Thanking and expressing regret, meeting people and taking leave of them	
9. Serving food	Food and utensils
10. Cleaning utensils	Utensils, rag and vim
11. Proper breathing, sitting, walking, eating and drinking	

3. Motor Development Activities

Activities	*Materials*
1. Pouring liquids	Glasses
2. Chopping vegetables and fruits	Knife, vegetables and fruits.
3. Sieving and cleaning wheat	Sieve and wheat
4. Shelling peas/beans	
5. Arranging flowers in a pot or vase	Flower vase, flowers
6. Sweeping and scrubbing floor	Broom, rags.
7. Dusting furniture	Duster
8. Folding clothes	
9. Putting things in order	

4. Activities for Language Development

Activities	*Materials*
1. Conversation	Topics
2. Recitation of nursery rhymes and singing of songs	Nursery rhyme-books, musical instruments.
3. Story telling	Story-books
4. Dramatics	Drama-books
5. Puppetry	Puppet theatre, puppets, etc.

6. Listening to recorded programme tapes, etc.	Gramophone records, tape recorders,
7. Viewing films, film-strips	Projector, film-strips and films.
8. Excursions and visits to museums, zoos, exhibitions, etc.	Cards, picture-books, scrap-books charts, display and boards
9. Developing readiness and beginning reading	Alphabetical letters or cards, vocabulary cards, reading materials

5. Activities for Mathematical Concept

Activities	*Materials*
1. Naming units of quantities numerical rods or broad stairs.	Things from the environment,
2. Recognising numerical symbols	Wooden or plastic numerical symbols, and sand paper, symbols, on cards, etc.
3. Associating symbols with quantities by means of cards	Objects and cards
4. Understanding the meaning of zero	Cards
5. Knowing odd and even numbers	Actual objects and cards
6. Naming and recognising coins	Coins of different values
7. Knowing names of geometrical shapes and recognising them	Geometrical shapes.
8. Knowing different measures like a kilo, 500 gms, 100 gms, 50 gms, litre, metre, hour, etc.	Weights, half litre bottles, wooden meter, measuring tape, etc.
9. Names of days and months	Calendar

6. Activities on Science Concepts

Activities	*Materials*
1. Bulk	Building blocks
2. Weight	Objects with same size but different weight such as pots, wooden pieces, stones, metal pieces, etc.
3. Forms and shapes	Regular and irregular shapes
4. Colours and shapes	Pairs of coloured things, colour boxes
5. Touch	Different types of cloth, sand paper, paper
6. Temperature	Hot and cold water, food, thermic sense material

7. Porosity	Earthen pots, blotting paper, sponge, dry earth
8. Compressibility	Balloon, rubber toys
9. Expansibility	Heated liquid
10. Elasticity	Rubber bands, elastic
11. Malleability	Clay plasticine
12. Gravity	Ball
13. Chemical changes	Wet cement, sugar and water, rusted iron material
14. Gases and liquids	Floating and non-floating toys, gas balloons.
15. Plant life	Plants, a patch of land, earch, manure
16. Animal life	Animals or a mini zoo

7. Aesthetic and Creative Activities

Activities	*Materials*
1. Cutting and pasting	Scissors, gum, pictures, glazed papers, albums
2. Paper folding	Papers, scissors
3. Toy making out of waste material	Waste material like bottle tops, shells, weeds, match-boxes, tea packets, soap, toffee-covers, cigarette cases, tins bottles, stones, nuts, etc.
4. Clay-modelling	Clay
5. Drawing and painting	Pencil, rubber, colours, drawing boards, brushes, etc.
6. Music	Musical instruments
7. Dancing	Bells, costumes, make-up materials, etc.
8. Dramatics	Theatre costumes, make-up materials, etc.
9. Puppetry	Puppets, theatre, accessories
10. Visits to exhibitions, museums	Transport facilities
11. Display of beautiful things in a cover	Beautiful things, display boards, shelves, racks, etc.

Equipment and Material for A Pre-School

Equipment is the material used in children's activities, both curricular (i.e., educational) and co-curricular (i.e., play). Play activities are very essential during early childhood. Materials used for play activities have been called "Play things" by Susan Issacs (1971). Young children in the beginning do not need many play things. Only selected few things may be provided to them. Variety may be added later as the children grow up. For pay the major equipment is the "toy which small children need to give expression to their spontaneous activities". The toys enable them to give outlet to their emotions. On the educational side, equipment provides a basis for activities and encourages the child for action. It also sharpens child's power of perception and extends his knowledge of world. The child also projects himself through the equipment which is very important for his affective development. Equipment also helps the child in his physical growth.

Characteristics of Equipment

The important thing about the equipment is not its quantity but quality and its suitability for the age group and the activities in which it is to be used. The aim of the schools should not be to accumulate a large number of equipment but they should be able to put it to use as Mialaret (1976) points out, "Schools that have large cupboards full of new or little used equipment are seldom good schools, whereas those that have simple equipment, shabby as a result of constant use, are often better educationally." The pre-school equipment should meet the following requirements.

1. *Physically Strong:* The equipment must be physically strong. The equipment which is easily broken and does not stand upto rough treatment may not be selected. It will prove costly as it will have to be replaced frequently.
2. *Attractive in Appearance:* The equipment may be attractive and pleasant to use. Though children may handle whatever material they are given, yet it is always better to give them things which are good in taste and possess aesthetic value. Such material can also be cheap.
3. *Multiple Use:* Given a new piece of equipment, a child will experiment with the new equipment putting it to use in many new activities.
4. *Proper Size:* As the children at the pre-school stage differ in age, they are at different stages of motor development and are, therefore, unable to grasp objects in the same way. Small children like large objects which they can clasp in their arms

but older children may take pleasure in handling smaller things.

5. *Meets Child's Needs:* The equipment must meet some of the basic needs of children and should not be forced on them. These needs include the need for activity, need for self-expression and need for personal creation.
6. *Serves Psychological and Intellectual Functions:* It should be seen that the equipment allows certain psychological and intellectual functions to come into play. As Mialaret Points out. "Certain classification games bring into action the fundamental psychological structures which are found in all intellectual activities. Thus the games children play with such equipment are of great educational value, since the child unconsciously organises his own experience, thus laying the foundation for logical thinking at a later stage."
7. *Provides Scope for Improvisation:* All equipment cannot be purchased for the pre-schools. Some of it should be prepared by the teachers out of such material as used tyres, ropes, empty cardboard boxes, locally available shells, sand, marble pieces, old bottles, match boxes, discarded pans and cans.

Categories of Equipment

Mialaret (1976) has listed different categories of equipment for use at the pre-school stage.

1. Ready Made Equipment: It may meet the requirement of children's immediate needs and be suitable for the activities organised by the teacher. But it is seldom functional and also cannot be put to multiple use. The qualities that are advertised for its sale are not always the ones that pre-school institutions consider it important.
2. Natural Equipment: This consists of objects collected and looked after by the pupils, teachers and even parents. Since these have been collected from child's environment, these are very easy to access.

REFERENCES

1. *Introduction to Early Childhood Education* – Jo Ann Brewer
2. *A Curriculum for the Pre-school Child Learning to Learn* – Audrey Curtis
3. *Innovations in Teaching-Learning Process* – Chauhan S.S.

4. *Teaching in the Early Years* – Bernard Spodek.
5. Eva L. Essa, *Introduction to Early Childhood Education* (3rd Ed.).
6. Muralidharan, R., & Banerji, U. *A Guide for Nursery School Teachers*, New Delhi: NCERT, 1969.
7. Issacs, S. (1929). *The Nursery Years*, London: Routledge and Kegan Paul.

9

France: Recent Developments in Care and Early Child Education (Since 1990)

As in most other European countries, the care and education of young children (aged 0-6) in France falls under two distinct rubrics: Children over two come under the administration of the educational system, whereas those under three pertain to the system of childcare. From the age of two, children can attend nursery school, but this is not mandatory.

Since 1990, there have been perceptible changes linked to the high unemployment rate, the deterioration of the economy, and the recent law on the Family (1994), which favours keeping children at home or placing them with a Childmindu. There is an observable declaration in the establishment of coaches and a rise in the number of childcare centres. Another change is the appearance of a number of innovative solution aimed at community development. Such as centres for freelance childminders, or parent child centres which brings together children and adults.

With regard to children over two in nursery school, recent changes have occurred more in the qualitative than the quantitative level. The attendance figures have remained stable for the past fifteen years or so (100% for children over 3 years and around 35 per cent for children aged two). With the implementation of the law on educational orientation (1989), primary schooling, in nursery and elementary school, is undertaken in cycles regrouping several classes. The aim is to provide better continuity in learning by tightening the links between nursery and elementary school. There are three cycles.

Cycle 1(Early Learning) Concerns the lower, middle and upper sections of nursery school (i.e., 2-5 years).

Cycle 2 (Basic Learning) concerns the upper section of nursery school and the two first classes of elementary school (5-8) years.

Cycle 3 (Reinforcements) relates to the three final classes of elementary school (9-11 years).

The programmes of 1995 confirm that nursery school is indeed school, even if the texts speak in terms of 'Spheres of activity' and 'learning tools' and favour the constraining and contextualising of these motions in a manner applicable to early learning. In 1990, university institutes for the training of school teachers setting up university degree courses for primary as well as secondary school teachers. The result is a marked distancing from the idea, originated in the early 1980's of an overall and unitary policy for young children. The only official text encouraging the closer association of pre-school services and professionals is a 1991 circular aiming to establish links between nursery school and other services. And, inservice training of a mixed nature is little known.

These recent developments have had their effect on research currently being done in the field.

Origins and Current Developments in Early Childhood Education Research

Contemporary research in early childhood education follows the path forged by a few pioneers whose thought is still very much alive.

Irene Lazine was a psychologist and a path-finder in the field of the 'psycho-pedagogy of infancy' (1964). Her educational proposals contributed significantly to the development of daycare centres and to their unshackling from the medical model on the 1960s, despite the general mistrust that reigned until the 1970's towards pacing children in collective settings.

The strong media presence of the psycho-analyst Francoise Dolto in the 'cause of children' (1985) found an echo among early childhood professionals, especially among education working in crèches and childcare centres. With the creation of the 'Green House' in Paris in 1979, she was a forerunner in the development of parent-child centres.

Pauline Keryomard is the best known among the common inspectors who were introducing teachers to new thinking on the education of young children.

Gastan Mialarel, has contributed to the elevation of the status of preschool education, in both the school careers of individuals and in school policy. In the 1960s the seminal work of historian Philippe Aries instigated a stream of important studies on the representation of childhood.

Since about 1970, infancy has become a fertile field of research, affecting a widening range of discipline - psychology, history, sociology, demography and economics.

In France traditional values in relation to schooling are concentrated on the notion of equal opportunity. More specifically, they are concerned with social class and with a handicapped and not, as in other countries, with gender or race.

The choice of methodology, on connection with the intellectual field, is also very diverse. All forms of action research are aiming simultaneously for the production of knowledge and the transformation of reality.

The Principle Themes Dealt with Today

The importance of the historical approach to the evolution of social definitions of early education and infant care is self-evident. It originated in France, developed by Aries (1960) as part of a series of works on the history of private life. The status of the young child in the family and in the society, early skills and learning, histories of games and play and of toys, etc. are the topics of historical investigations.

The monopolisation of crèches by the middle and upper classes during the 1970s and especially the 1980s appears to have slackened in recent years.

The studies conducted during 1980s on the effect of schooling of two-year olds reveals that it had a general positive impact on children's development in school and on their later achievements.

Daycare centres are currently enjoying success as a result of their transformation, over the last twenty years, from stop-gap rescue provision to contexts for living and learning.

"*Interactive Pedagogy*", a product of action research in the fields of pre-school and school education, is now promulgated through inservice training for teachers and other infancy professionals. Among the trainers are the practitioners who participated in the initial research. Among the most studied activities of nursery school, oral and written language is the object of special attention enquiries have been made into the efficacy of new technologies for language acquisition and to development of meta-reflective skills.

Research Policies: Institutions and Finance

Unlike other countries, France has no research centres specially oriented towards early childhood, only a range of organisation which encompass research in this field within their sphere of activity. Educational science, as taught in universities, leads to a degree but not to a professional qualification. The professional qualification for teachers requires a candidate to follow a two-year course provided in the IUFMs (Institute Universitaires de Formation des Maitres). In May 1995, a National Committee for the coordination of education research was created to conduct a regular stocktaking of research in the field, to compare it with research conducted abroad, and to suggest new projects and evaluate their success. Projects are also conducted within or between certain government ministries.

The Social Security Bureau for Aid to Families with Dependent Children (CNAF) also plays an important role in researches. Generally speaking, policy-makers rely on the results of research, for the elaboration of policies which will later be evaluated, once more, by researchers. The place given to early childhood in teacher training courses is itself very limited.

REFERENCES

1. Butts, R. Freeman. (1955). *A Cultural History of Western Education.* New York: McGraw-Hill Book, Co., Inc.
2. Eva L. Essa, *Introduction to Early Childhood Education* (3rd ed.).
3. Austin, Gilbert R. *Early Childhood Education.* An International Perspective, New York: Academic Press, 1976.

10

Pre-School Groups in America Today

In the United States today many families recognise the values of groups preliminary to elementary school, and reach out for them. In nursery school or Kindergarten, pre-school children have a group experience which extends the values of family life, giving them a total experience in democratic living in which cooperation is strengthened and competition minimised.

The present day increase in nursery and kindergarten groups is influenced by several factors which shape family living and society itself. These include,

- Development of suburban living
- Mechanisation in the home
- Increased numbers of women at work outside the home
- Increased community assumption of responsibility for families
- Educators sensitivity to the social order and to family needs

Business Recognises Pre-School Groups

Manufacturers of baby food, children's clothing, toys and other items for the pre-school child are aware of the pre-school group as a vehicle for consumer education. Local merchants as well as industries that are national in scope are willing to sponsor morning pre-school programmes on TV to advertise their mechandise.

States Recognise Pre-school Groups

As the number of pre-school group has increased, states have taken greater responsibility for them, defining limits within which they must operate. These limits are designed to safeguard the health and safety of the children and to provide for their education as future citizens. State differ in the amount and kind of educational guidance they give to pre-school groups. Through the consulting service as the licensing procedure of the state Department of Social Welfare, pre-school groups throughout California are continuously encouraged to improve their programmes.

Those responsible for day nurseries are expected to plan for the child in terms of:

1. His own family and secure place in it—the mature love of his parent.
2. An opportunity to grow and develop psychologically, spiritually, emotionally, intellectually and socially at his own pace.
3. Sympathetic and understanding help in the growing process.
4. Protection from hazards he is too young to face alone.

Schools Foster Pre-school Groups

School systems which recognise the importance of the family as a social unit have pre-school groups tied into their programmes at several points. In some communities, formal schooling begins with four-year old children. In many communities, kindergarten is the first school experience. High school home economics programmes which prepare students for family living and care of children operate nursery schools as laboratories in which the students observe and participate. Adult education programmes provide an opportunity for parents to observe their children in group situations, then to discuss their observations; to participate in parent discussions and lecture forums under able leadership; and to participate in education of their children are in a pre-school group.

Colleges and universities which prepare nursery, elementary, and high school teachers and leaders for home economics, child development, and adult education programmes also make nursery school or kindergarten observation and participation available to their students. They recognise that those who are to work with families need to have experience with pre-school children.

What Families Benefit from Pre-school Groups?

The pre-school groups which meet regularly throughout the school year are attended primarily by children whose families do not find it inconvenient to get them to the group. The location of a pre-school group is an important factor in determining what families it will serve.

Pre-school groups may be classified according to the age level of the children they serve, according as to whether they are laboratory schools, and according to the kind of family need they meet. Kindergarten are for five year-old children's nursery groups are for three and four-year old children.

The variety of pre-school groups developed during and after World War I, where all pre-school groups benefited from the new work opportunities for women. The first parent-cooperative nursery school in the United States was organised during the war period by a group of mothers interested in "Social education for their children, parent education for themselves, and a little free time for Red Cross Work."

The Post-World War I period saw the rapid development of several kinds of pre-school groups, including laboratory groups, designed to help students learn about normal young children.

Day Nurseries

The day nurseries of the city are supported by the community chest, endowments, and donations, and fees based on the size of the family, their income and their ability to pay. The aim of the day nurseries is "to provide a happy, healthy and understanding environment in which a child may grow and develop during the time his own parents are unable to care for him."

Childcare Centres

Childcare centres are supported by funds provided by the state (two-thirds) and by fees graduated according to family income (one-third). In the California City of 250,000 eleven childcare centres are available, under the supervision of the local school district. Childcare centres endeavour to reach the low-income families and other families who need their services. The children from broken homes in the city atten a nursery group when someone responsible for them makes arrangements for them to attend. Children in many families under financial stress are enrolled by their parents in the day nursery and childcare centres available through welfare channels.

Private Nursery Schools and Kindergartens

Families at the higher end of the economic scale in the city enroll their children in private pre-school groups supported entirely by fees. These groups are convenient families in which the mother has a job, club or social activities or other personal interests.

Church-Sponsored Groups for Preschool Children

The policies of a church-sponsored pre-school group determine what and how many families it will serve, and are subject to review by the governing board of the church. At worst, the board may oppose the use of church facilities by pre-school children; at best, it may supplement fees with funds to be used to improve equipment and to increase the amount of teaching time in relation to the number of children in the school.

School-Affiliated Pre-school Groups

It has been pointed out that the pre-school groups in adult education programmes are primarily for the education of the parents, and are generally available to the families of all pre-school children. The groups are attended by children and parents of families who are sufficiently interested in their children to make the effort to come regularly as often as the group meets. The pre-school groups that are an integral part of schools designed to prepare future parents and teachers are more selective and have limited enrolments. Often parents are members of the school faculty or students in the college.

Parent-Cooperative Group

Families who wish to share the pre-school experience of their children form parent-cooperative groups. In the city studied, there are twenty-one such groups. They meet in the city part in church, or in community centres. Each children's group meets two, three, or four mornings a week-depending upon the age of the children and the planning of their parents and teacher. Cooperative nurseries help children develop through democratic and constructive play situations. Mothers cooperate in providing regular supervised play for their pre-school children.

Backyard Play Groups

Backyard groups form when several neighbourhood families with pre-school children find it useful to have their children play together regularly. When these informal groups meet in a backyard well equipped for children, or at a playground area, the number of conflict situations among the children is less than when they are expected to play in an environment that has little to stimulate constructive activities.

Backyard groups differ from the organised groups in that they do not have one mother figure but a succession of them. For the children, this discontinuity in their experience is much like having a series of babysitters who reappear from time to time.

The Role of the Pre-school Teacher

The teacher in the pre-school group, like the mother in the home, is the person responsible for creating an atmosphere of love. The empathy of the teacher with each person, and the empathy among persons is a measure of the love that permeates the pre-school group.

Plans a Balanced Curriculum

Teachers should prepare the activities for well-rounded physical development of child. Three and four-year old children are to develop control of their large muscles. The teacher should help the children to develop an understanding of the various roles they have and will have in the society, she should introduce them to quantitative as well as qualitative relationships and values as they move themselves through space.

Further Development of Parents

The teacher who creates an atmosphere of love in which the children develop socially, emotionally, physically and intellectually also creates an atmosphere favourable to the development of the parents and prospective parents who observe or participate in the pre-school group. As they experience the comfortable feeling of the children's group, they become aware of the combination of a love, democratic procedure and educational technique, which produce it.

Interprets the Pre-school Group to the Community

Realising the importance of pre-school group experience, the teacher should help other members of the community to appreciate how the pre-school group strengthens and enriches family life. The teacher who is aware of the various types of pre-school groups can advise families who are looking for the group especially suited for their family.

Through membership in such professional organizations as the National Association for Nursery Education and the Association for Childhood Education International, the teacher has the opportunity to work with others who are interested in pre-school children. The teachers should be primarily concerned that pre-school groups be planned in terms of children of pre-school age and in terms of families as they are today.

In what ways can children develop in a pre-school group development as a person

The child's experience in a pre-school group should faster his development in every day. This development may be described as having four aspects: social, intellectual, physical, and emotional.

(a) Social Development

As a child goes from his home into a nursery group, into kindergarten and on into the primary grades and the elementary school, he moves into atmospheres of gradually increasing formality and more rigidly structured programmes of activities. This increase in structuring parallels his social development. As he learns to be part of a group, he is able to participate in group activities for longer periods of time.

(b) Intellectual Development

Today it is evident that all aspects of the elementary school curriculum have their roots in the nursery group and kindergarten. He learns at his age level what will be a foundation for his later learning about health, social studies, science, mathematics, language, art and music.

(c) Physical Development

A pre-school group should give an aid to the well-rounded physical development of children. Apparatus helps them to learn how to climb and how to handle their bodies in different positions. The good teacher analyses the kind of play children have in their community and plans activities designed to supplement their play.

Emotional Development

Teachers of nursery groups and kindergartens must be aware of the importance of making daily provision for helping children to find suitable emotional outlets, to find pleasure in socially acceptable behaviour and to experience genuine love. Only the home is more important in furthering desirable emotional development.

REFERENCES

1. Butts, R. Freeman. (1955). *A Cultural History of Western Education.* New York: McGraw-Hill Book, Co., Inc.
2. Eva L. Essa, *Introduction to Early Childhood Education* (3rd Ed.).
3. Austin, Gilbert R. *Early Childhood Education.* An International Perspective, New York: Academic Press, 1976.
4. *The Years before School–Guiding Pre-school Children*–Vivian Edmiston Todd, Helen Hefferman.
5. UNESCO, *New Approaches to Education of Children of Pre-School Age Report of a Regional Meeting of Experts*, Bangkok, UNESCO Regional Office for Education in Asia and Oceania, 1979.

11

Elementary School Facilities in India and Iran

One of the most provocative and compelling questions regarding school facilities is the influence of the educational environment has upon performance of students and teachers. Common belief held by educators is that the facilities do indeed have an influence upon how well students and teachers perform. Considerable research has taken place in the United States and European Countries to assess the possible relationship between student performance and school facilities. Researchers have launched studies to investigate the influence of various school facilities components such as library, laboratory, size and age of school building, the presence or absence of windows in classrooms, air-conditioning, space allocation per pupil, hygienic facilities (like safe water, soap), noice level, thermal conditions and furniture types upon student performance in an effort to discover a relationship. A review of literature supports the premise that when school facilities use well designed and maintained they can enhance the learning environment for students, teachers and the community (O'Neill, 2000).

Many studies have explored the relationship between school conditions and achievement-related behaviour (c.f. McGuffey, 1982; Burnett, 1995, Rivera-Batiz and Marti, 1995). For example, Lemasters, (1997) reviewed several recent studies on the influence of school conditions on academic achievement. All the studies found the same relationship, in varying degrees schools facilities and student achievement. However, researchers who have studied school facilities and teaching and learning process have found some interesting relationships.

A survey of overcrowded schools in New York city found that 75 per cent of teachers indicated that overcrowding affects classroom activities and 70 per cent of teachers indicated that overcrowding affected their instructional techniques (Rivera Batiz and Marti, 1995). Corcoran, Walker and White (1988) found that overcrowding, as well as heavy teacher work loads, created stressful working conditions for teachers that led to higher teacher absenteeism.

Bowers and Burkett (1988) conducted that a relationship did exist between the physical environment and student achievement, health, attendance and behaviour. In their study Dobbelsteen, Levin and Oosterbeck (1998) revealed that class size has a highly significant and positive effect on school performance. Earthman (1998) found that building condition did affect student achievement. Edwards, (1992) investigated the relationship between parental involvement, school building condition and student achievement in schools in Washington, DC. The condition of public school buildings is affected by parental involvement and that the condition of the school building further affects student achievement. In recent study, Philips (1997) found significant differences in the reading and arithmetic scores between students in new buildings and students in old buildings. Cervantes (1999) tried to examine the relationship between the school building condition and academic achievement and behaviour of students who are enrolled in Grades 4, 7 and 11 in selected Alabama public schools.

Findings indicated a relationship between maths achievement and the building category school site, in Grade II, across all schools. The relationship between the reading achievement and the building category of school site was noted.

Finally, lack of adequate school facilities also result in conditions that compromise student safety. Students who attend schools in poor condition may be exposed to such health threats as poor air quality, hazardous material and sewage overflows. In more extreme cases, student may also be put in more immediate physical danger when parts of the buildings collapse or when safety features (e.g. fire alarms, sprinkler systems) fail. However the main purpose of this study is a comparison between elementary school facilities in two developing countries — India and Iran.

The main findings of the study (Abbasi, 2004) are:

- The number of government schools in Iran is more than in India.
- In Iran the number of schools with new buildings was more than in India.
- Indian schools do not have adequate classrooms and classrooms are overcrowded.
- The number of staff room and principal's room is more in India than in Iran.
- More than 1/3 of Indian schools have no sufficient numbers of teachers.

In any country, before a school becomes operational, the infrastructure must be adequate. The advantage of this is that it creates an enabling teaching environment. Usually in many developing countries, elementary schools do not have adequate facilities. In Philippines the conditions of most school buildings are very poor. (World Bank 2001). In Tajikistan, absolute poverty and dilapidated school facilities are the major reasons for an increasing percentage of children not attending school (UNICEF, 2002). Nasir, and Nazli (2000) reported that in Pakistan the low enrolment rates at the primary level, wide disparities between regions and gender, lack of trained teachers, deficiency of proper teaching materials and poor physical infrastructure of schools indicate the poor performance of education sector in economy. In Vietnam, many children living in rural areas, especially ethnic minorities lack access to clean, hygienic and safe school facilities (UNICEF, 2002).

In India research conducted by Sarma (1992) highlighted the fact that physical facilities of schools in District of Sibsagar were for from satisfactory. 80 per cent of schools in her study had a single hall with no partition between the classes, 90 per cent had no urinals and 60 per cent had no provision of drinking water facility. In Iran, Fallahi (1993) found that for expansion of schools and school facilities, the government has not been able to overcome these shortages mainly due to the weak economy, which is result of eight years war with Iraq.

According to Nazari (1994) each school has four kinds of spaces, which are educational, training, administrative and hygienic.

The findings of study by Parvin Abbasi Regional Institute of Education, Mysore reveal that in India (Mysore) average age of school building in 38 years, whereas average age of Iranian schools in 20 years. In addition 60 per cent of Indian Headmasters/Head mistresses said that their schools do not have adequate classrooms. Data regarding the age of schools and their condition suggests that the oldest schools are more and they need attention but may of these schools do not have plans for improvement. The data also suggest that schools have a problem with overcrowding. A substantial number of schools are in poor condition, and some of them suffer from lack of adequate educational facilities. Findings of this study support research by Sarma, (1992), NCERT (1999) and Rao and Cheng (2001) who found that Indian Elementary schools do not have sufficient facilities to prepare a good environment for teachers and students. However, this study found that facilities of schools were for from satisfactory and more investment is needed to improve conditions of schools.

In fact without adequate resources to initiate schools rehabilitation, appropriate learning conditions for children cannot be provided.

Finally, lack of adequate school facilities may also result in conditions that compromise student safety. Students who attend schools in poor condition may be exposed to such health threats as poor air quality, hazardous materials, and sewage overflows. The overall comparison indicates that Iranian elementary schools are better equipped than Indian schools.

REFERENCE

1. Abbasi, P. (2004). *Elementary School Facilities in India and Iran.* Edutracks.

12
Development of Early Childhood Education in United Kingdom

Early childhood education research in the UK has been dominated by child development research and the traditions of psychology. Despite the efforts of the early pioneers (e.g.: Owen, Pestalozzi, Froebel, Montessori, McMillan and Isaacs). Nursery provision in this country was remained neglected while other European states were setting up their near universal systems. Prior to the end of the 1960s, there were very few textbooks for students of primary or early years of education. Between the two World Wars, Susan Isaacs had been appointed to a post in child development at the London University Institute and here books formed the core of those training to work in the early years. While, at that time American developmental psychologists were dominating the world with ideas about children's universal developmental progression irrespective of culture and society.

In 1965 an influential paper by Douglas and Ross (1965) was published claiming that children who had attained nursery provision gained cognitively and emotionally. With the publication of the Plowden Report (1967) interest in early childhood grew because policymakers were looking for best practice attempting to measure effectiveness, in the hope that early inputs would remedy any under achievement caused by disadvantage. The type of research which has been regarded as most desirable in UK, has generally been based on positivistic, natural science models.

John and Elizabeth Newson (1965) adopted an interpretive paradigm, attempting to provide information about the lives of young children growing up in an urban society, co-constructing their worlds together with their families.

In 1974, a review of current early childhood education research (Tizard, 1974) was published. The review had arisen in response to a government announcement of 1972, that nursery provision was to be substantially increased, commenting that in most other European countries, there had already been an expansion of services for young children, Barbara Tizard adds that the increase in provision had been mooted for two main reasons. Firstly, the growing number of mothers wishing or needing to continue in employment outside the home, and secondly, the view that some children begin school at a disadvantage as a result of family variables, and that an expansion of public provision would compensate for this, leading to higher levels of achievement at primary and secondary school. Here review categorised contemporary projects into the following research groupings.

1. Research concerned with the pre-school, research with young children at home.
2. Topics such as cognitive skills, evaluation of services, education and development of young children with severe learning difficulties.
3. Social disadvantage.
4. Other problems, such as early school socialisation, transition, general provision of services, staff training.

In 1972, a study by Davie, Butler and Golstein was published, revealing the widening gulf during the school years between children born in poverty and those born into affluence. Margaret Clark, who also conducted a survey of research evidence in the 1980s, points out that the economic and psychological ethos of the 1960s had not been conducive to the expansion of pre-school provision, because of the shortage of teachers for older children, and because of the powerful impact of findings about maternal deprivation.

Many of the studies which were funded in the wake of the proposals to extend pre-school provision in the UK seem to have been preoccupied with measurable variables such as the length of the day in the setting, the number of children in a group, the length of time in nursery and their effects on a child's progress as measured by intelligence tests. Other complicating factors in the UK include the variety of pre-school provision, much of it relatively unregulated, and much of it seen as either social or socio emotional.

In one study began in 1970, some 13,135 children were traced and data collected about them at birth, at five years old and again at then, when they were interviewed. The project provided the field with comparisons of children's achievements following attendance at different types of pre-school provision. The largest project currently under this way is led by Kathy Sylva begun when she was professor of Child Development and Primary Education at the London University Institute of Education. This project continues in the tradition of searching for the characteristics of the most effective pre-school provision. In addition, Emeritus Professor, Colwyn Trevartheris work is highly regarded for the support it gives to theories about the need for interaction and meaning making in early childhood.

Pre-school Activities in England

Given below is a list of activities enjoyed by nursery school children of Children's Centre of University of Leeds.

Home Corner Play: Although manufactured furniture and equipment is very attractive, strong simple furniture can be cheaply made from wooden boxes. Gaily coloured dressing-up clothes should be included in the home corner, and plenty of space in which dramatic play can develop.

Painting: Finger painting, poster painting.

Drawing: Crayoning, chalking, using felt pens and charcoal.

Water play: Out of doors whenever possible, watering the garden, blowing bubbles, bathing the baby, washing clothes, and mixing sand and water.

Sand Play: Wet and Dry sand, opportunity to cart sand from one place to another, to combine sand play with pulley and builder play and to mix up sand and water.

Clay: Pounding and moulding red or white clay on boards, play with dough, leading to simple pastry making.

Wood work: Use of hammers, nails, a tenon saw, fairly soft wood and wooden boxes of any kind, wooden wheels, hooks, etc., add to

(*b*) Find the difference among pictures.
(*c*) Arrange objects according to their size, shape, etc.
(*d*) Observe plants growing animals moving, people working, day and night, clouds, rain, etc.
(*e*) Touch, feel, taste and smell things.

Concepts must be taught to children in a specific sequence, i.e. from simple to complex. Songs, stories, games, free conversation, etc. can be used for teaching the concept.

Creative Activities

Creative activities include cutting, pasting, painting, drawing, printing, folding, clay modeling, etc.

How to do it?

(*a*) Divide children in small groups
(*b*) Each group should be given a different activity
(*c*) Give enough material so that each child has something to do
(*d*) Show children what they have to do
(*e*) Avoid giving models for children to copy
(*f*) Allow them to express their own imagination or creativity
(*g*) Praise efforts of all children
(*h*) Interchange the activities within group

Talk to Children

(*a*) Seat children in the semi circle
(*b*) Sit on the floor
(*c*) Keep you voice clear and soft
(*d*) Initiate the conservation by asking questions
(*e*) Wait for the response
(*f*) Give each child a chance to speak
(*g*) Listen to each ones speech
(*h*) Praise their efforts

Sing A Song

(*a*) Sing songs in tune
(*b*) Use a simple musical instrument
(*c*) Sing the song slowly and ensure each child repeats after you

(*d*) Sing songs that have plenty of scope for action
(*e*) Introduce variety by changing tunes, beat and words.

For Psychomotor Development

Activities like walking, running, hopping, rolling, jumping, crawling, stretching and bending, are there.

Affective Development

Dramatisation

Make children dramatise stories, songs, events, birds, animals, etc., allow them to dress up and act according to their own imagination, ensure children share the material with each other.

Organisation of pre-school Learning

Since children grow, develop and learn through play, the entire programme and the environment of pre-school should be built around play. So plan the daily programme in the pre-school in such a way as to achieve the objective, namely the all-round development of the child.

The thematic approach presents the possibility of an extremely useful and enjoyable pre-school programme it is essentially for meeting their development needs.

Thematic Approach

Different themes related to the immediate environment of the child are related e.g.: trees, animals, birds, flowers, insects, etc. Various activities are developed around the themes and used at the centre. Normally each theme is used for a week. During that week, children are involved various activities related to that particular theme. All basic concepts like size, shape, colour, number, space, position, etc. can be brought out using the theme, but it is also all to form concepts in relation to the self and the environment.

This approach provides planned opportunities for joyful and meaningful learning and prepare him/her for entering primary school. The methodology used here is child-oriented. Themes selected should be from the child's immediate surroundings and at the comprehension level 3 to 6 years old children. While developing activities the child should not be over-burdened with too much information.

Non formal media such as free conversation, stories, puppetry, arts, crafts, dance, etc. may be used to highlight the significant aspects of each theme keeping play as the primary medium.

Possible themes are trees, vegetables, birds, etc. The most important requirement of the thematic approach is effective planning by the teacher for time, space, equipment and materials.

Planning the Daily Timetable

The daily routine should be so planned as to meet the needs of the children. Select at least 1 or 2 activities meant to help in each aspect of the child's development. A balanced programme will include something for body, social adjustment, mind, creative expression, senses, emotion, curiosity, etc.

For children, the whole programme has one major purpose play and fun. Planning should be made in the making of the timetable. Care should be given to impart individual and group activities.

Planning the Use of Space

Children need space for physical movement and activity, an environment that stimulates variety and change.

A large open space in the centre of the room as well as a scattering of smaller spaces is needed. Children can be seated in smaller groups for different activities. For the mid day meal children can sit in the centre of the room. A verandah or courtyard is ideal.

Planning Equipments and Materials

Equipments are to be made simple. It includes out door play equipments, furniture, storage, kitchen equipments, etc.

Evaluation of Children

The first aim of evaluation should be to facilitate progress in all aspects of the child's development - physical, emotional, social and mental a record may be maintained for each child to enable the teacher to note the stages of progress.

Advantages of Thematic Approach

(*a*) It gives the teacher a sense of direction and provides here with enough scope to plan and prepare.

(b) It provides scope for a variety of creative activity and an adaptive frame of work.

(c) It promotes a sense of healthy competition among the teachers at various pre-school centres.

(d) There is scope for systematic monitoring and evaluation of the programme.

(e) It caters the developmental needs of the child and prepares him/her for the primary school.

REFERENCES

1. *Early Childhood Care and Education*—U.K. Rao.
2. *Primary Schooling in India*—Amarjeet, Sinha.
3. Govt. of India, *Education and National Development the Report of Education Commission*, New Delhi: Manager of Publications, 1966. pp. 149-151.
4. Rawat, D.S. (1970) *Pre-Primary Teacher Education Curriculum*. New Delhi: NCERT.
5. Department of Education and Science (1989). *School Teacher Appraisal*—A National Framework. Report of the National Steering Group on the School Teacher Appraisal, Pilot Study, MHSO, London.
6. *Introduction to Early Childhood Education*—Jo Ann Brewer.

14

Organisation of Curriculum at Elementary Stage

The basic features and main thrusts of the new curricular framework could be visualised as follows:

1. Emphasis on the development of human resources to put the young men and women of India on the fore front of development for the realisation of the national goals of education, prosperity and social cohesion.
2. Broad-based general education to all learners at the elementary (5 years of primary and 3 years of UP) and secondary (2 years) stages.
3. A broad-based common scheme of studies for the elementary and secondary stages with emphasis on the skill of "learning how to learn."
4. The 1976 addition to the constitution of India laid down some fundamental duties which exhorted all Indian citizens to:

   (*a*) abide by the constitution and respect its ideals and institutions, the National Flag and the National Anthem
   (*b*) Cherish and follow the noble ideals that inspired our national struggle for freedom
   (*c*) Uphold and protect the sovereignty unity and integrity of the country.
   (*d*) Defend the country and render national service when called up on to do so.
   (*e*) Promote harmony and the spirit of common brotherhood among all the people of India.
   (*f*) Renounce practices derogatory to the dignity of women.

5. The common core components comprise:

    a) The history of India's freedom movement
    b) The constitutional obligations
    c) Content essential to nurture national identity
    d) India's common cultural heritage
    e) Egalitarianism, democracy and secularism
    f) Equality of sexes
    g) Protection and preservation of the environment
    h) Removal of social barriers
    i) Observance of the small family norm
    j) Inculcation of scientific temper

6. Emphasis on ensuring to minimum essential level of acquisition of knowledge, understanding and skill in all subjects at all stages.
7. Provision of flexibility in terms of selection of content/ components and learning experiences.
8. Emphasis on learner centred and activity based processes rather than the teacher-centred content-based approach during curriculum transaction.
9. Recasting of the examination system and introduction of continuous and comprehensive evaluation that incorporates both scholastic and non-scholastic aspects of education.
10. Provision of remedial teaching as well as counselling services for carrying out the diagnosis of learning problems.
11. Setting up an appropriate system of National Testing Service (NTS) for the selection and development of norms of comparable competence across the nation.
12. Applicability of the curriculum to all learners irrespective of their modes/channels of learning.
13. Provision of essential facilities or the minimum conditions for learning through effective transaction of curriculum in all schools.

Minimum Levels of Learning (MLL)

Minimum Levels of Learning or essential levels of learning outcomes has been introduced in order to bring about a broad commonality in the standard of education throughout the country.

The concept of MLLs is not fragmentary, but holistic in nature.

'Learning' is to be taken in the broad sense of 'Skill', 'quality', 'attitude' and 'value' too. In that sense, the term would embrace all the cognitive, psycho-motor and affective area learning outcomes of education.

While emphasis has been laid on the introduction of the norms of MLLs and adoption of a common scheme of studies at different stages of school education, flexibility is envisaged in the selection of strategy for curriculum transaction, in order to make learning more relevant to the needs and environmental contests of the learners.

Scheme of Studies

A common scheme of studies is advocated for classes I to X. The emphasis would shift from factual knowledge to the process of understanding, thinking and internalising. Besides, personality development, value education, health and physical education, art education and work experience should be given appropriate importance in the school curriculum.

***(a) Pre-Primary Education* (2 years)**

This stage of education would help children prepare for school later through group activities, play-way techniques, language games, number games and activities directed to promote socialisation and environmental awareness. Perception, pleasure and participation are to be emphasised.

No formal teaching of subjects or reading and writing are to be undertaken at this stage.

***(b) Elementary Education* (8 years)**

Primary Stage (5 Years)

A. Classes I and II

(i) One language—the home language/ the regional language
(ii) Mathematics
(iii) Environmental studies
(iv) The three areas of work education, arts (fine and performing), and health activities may be put together and a suitable name may be given to them.

B. Classes III-V

(i) One language-home language/regional language
(ii) English
(iii) Mathematics
(iv) Environmental Studies
(v) Work education, arts (Fine and Performing), Health activities.

Upper Primary Stage (3 years)

(i) Three languages
(ii) Mathematics
(iii) Science and Technology
(iv) Social Sciences
(v) Work Education, Art Education (Fine and Performing), and Health and Physical Education (including NCC, Scouts and Guides)

Primary Stage

The study of social sciences begins formally from class I. It should be called 'Environmental Sciences'. In Class I and II children should be introduced to the environment as a whole without making a clear cut distinction between natural and human elements. In classes III to V children should be introduced to the natural and human aspects of the environment. Stories and narratives concerning everyday life, work, leisure and culture in the past, e.g., food, clothes, houses, transport, work, etc. should be given to children. They should be able to question and record, and to communicate ideas and information by the end of class V.

Upper Primary Stage

At this stage, the issues/themes identified earlier and drawn from history, geography, economics, civics and sociology should comprise the study of social sciences. The learner at this stage should be initiated into the study of India's past by selecting important/major events/episodes and developments—social, cultural and scientific in a chronological order and by making inks among them as also the cultural heritage.

The learners should be helped to understand and appreciate some of the ancient civilisation of the world and their interconnections as well as some major historical developments of the world.

The students should be able to investigate and undertake studies on their own concerning simple questions.

The diversities in land and people and their interdependence, the contemporary society-social, political and economic in situations and their functioning, globalisation and liberalisation and its impact, etc. may help students understand the social economic and political issues in the right perspective. Use of Information Technology should be promoted in studying social sciences.

Formulation of Objectives

In curriculum organisation formulation of objectives has a significant place because these play a fundamental role in determining the content, strategies and evaluation as components of the curriculum cycle. The overall objectives of curriculum would coincide with the overall aim of education.

General Objectives of Education

School curriculum should help to generate and promote among the learners:

1. Language abilities: (listening, speaking, reading and writing) needed for social living and further learning.
2. Communication Skills (verbal and visual) for effective participation in day-to-day activities.
3. Mathematical abilities to develop a logical mind and enable learners to perform simple mathematical operations and their application in every day life.
4. Scientific temper characterised by spirit of enquiry, courage to question and objectivity leading to elimination of obscurantism, superstition and fatalism.
5. Knowledge of Scientific methods of enquiry and its use in solving problems.
6. Understanding of the environment in its totality (natural and social and their interactive processes), the environmental problems and the ways and means to preserve the environment.
7. Abilities to investigate into various issues and problems at

the local, regional, national and global levels and to make one's own independent assessment.

8. Appreciation of sacrifices and contributions made by the freedom fighters and social workers in India's freedom struggle and social regeneration, and readiness to follow their ideals.
9. Qualities that make a person humane and socially effective, giving meaning and direction to life. These values may be clustered around social/economic and personal/spiritual values.
10. Understanding the diversity in lands and people living, in different parts of the country and the country's composite cultural heritage.
11. Appreciation for the need of a balanced synthesis between the change oriented technologies and the continuity of the country's traditions and heritage.
12. Knowledge of and respect for our national symbols and desire and determination to uphold the ideals of national identity and unity.
13. Understanding the positive and the negative impact of the processes of globalisation, liberalisation and localisation in the context of our own country.
14. Knowledge, attitude and habits necessary for keeping physically and mentally fit and strong in conformity with the normal developmental pattern.
15. An awareness of the inherent equality of all and the need for global fraternity with a strong commitment to human values and to social justice.
16. Application of an readiness to practice in life the national goals of socialism, secularism, healthy democracy and non-violence.
17. Qualities and characteristics necessary for self-learning, self-directed learning and lifelong learning leading to the creation of a learning society.
18. Pre-vocational/vocational skills, willingness to work hard, entrepreneurship and dignity of manual work necessary for increasing productivity, obtaining job-satisfaction and creating wealth generating systems.
19. Ability to discover and appreciate beauty in different life situations, and integrate it into one's own personality.

20. Capacity not only to accumulate factual information but also to understand, reflect and internalise and develop insight.
21. Capability of appreciating and tolerating differences and diversities of various sorts/ideologies and the capacity to chose between alternative value systems.
22. Appreciation of various consequences of large families and over population and need for checking population growth; and
23. Cultivating proper understanding of and attitude toward healthy sex related issues and healthy, respectful attitude toward members of the opposite sex.

REFERENCES

1. *A Curriculum for the Pre-school Child Learning to Learn* – Audrey Curtis
2. Eva L. Essa, *Introduction to Early Childhood Education* (3rd Ed.).
3. MacDonald, James B. *A Proper Curriculum for Young Children*, Phi Delta Kappa 50, No. 7, (March 1969): 406.
4. Rawat, D.S. (1970) *Pre-Primary Teacher Education Curriculum*. New Delhi: NCERT.

15

State Level Bodies on Elementary Education

SCERT- Role and Functions

The State Institute of Education (SIEs) were established during the mid-sixties in the country to work for qualitative improvement of elementary education through organisation of inservice training for teachers and supervisors, execution of research and extension activities, and development of instructional materials.

SCERT's-Development and Present Status

The Government of India initiated a scheme for setting up the State Institute of Education in different states as far back as 1963 for qualitative improvement of school education in general and elementary teacher education in particular. Though initially only major states started these institutions, many other followed suit in view of the need for such academic institutions to coordinate all academic projects in every state or union territory.

Subsequently, in the course of time, in some states, specialised institutes/agencies/units were established in some other specific areas like Science education, English language teaching, educational technology, vocational guidance and counselling, etc. In 1973, the Ministry of Education and Social Welfare recommended that all such existing institutions or various units in the State Education Department be merged into a single organisation and designated as the State Council of Educational Research and Training (SCERT). In some states the nomenclature of SIEs remained the same but with increased functions and responsibilities.

SCERTs/SIEs have been set up in almost all the states/Union Territories (UT's) in the country. Four the UTs namely Pondicheri, Daman and Diu, Dadar and Nagar Haveli and Lakshadweep have neither an SCERT not SIE. However the academic functions in these UTs are being looked after by the academic wings of State Education Departments or State Training Centres, of these some have bee recently upgrades as DIETs.

The academic activities and programmes is an SCERT are carried out by its various departments/Units/Wings. Generally, the SCERT is headed by a Director who is assisted by the officers and subject specialists/Technical Assistants. The question of providing autonomous status to the SCERTs are envisaged in the scheme, is being pursued in many states/UTs.

The Changing Role of SCERT's

NPE 1986 and POA envisaged additional role and functions for the SCERT's. SCERTs is expected to guide support and assist the state education department in its mission to improve the quality of school education and teacher education. It will also function as the state resource institution to provide academic support to all stages of school education from pre-primary to senior secondary stage of education. SCERT's have the mandate to supervise and support DIET's in order to facilitate their operationalisation and effective functioning.

Types of Activities and Programmes of SCERT's

1. *Research*

The staff members are expected to conduct research studies related to the significant educational problems of the state to improve the quality of elementary, secondary and teacher education. Besides they are conduct status studies and educational surveys to get benchmark data and develop information system related to school education and teacher education in the state policy planning and management.

2. *Development*

The development of curricular policies, syllabi and insuructional material, print and non-print both for formal and non-formal education system and come under the purview of the SCERT's. The

SCERT's/SIE's may under take the task of developing criterion for inspection and supervision of elementary schools at block level.

3. *Training*

- Continuing education of teachers, supervisors, and other educational personnel.
- Plan, implement, monitor and evaluate all pre-service and inservice teacher education, particularly at elementary level in the state.
- Short/long duration inservice training/orientation programmes for school teachers, master trainers and resource persons with the help of DIET's.
- Familiarise the DIET faculty with the latest technology for organising inservice education of teachers.

4. *Extension*

SCERT is expected to function as a think-tank of the State Department of Education to promote innovations and action research for improved practices in school education and teacher education. For this, the SCERT should organise workshops for school teachers and the DIET faculty to guide them to design action research projects and evolve/replicate innovative practices to improve classroom teaching and other institutional programmes.

In house staff development activities - seminars, talks, conferences research colloquia, panel discussions, extension lectures on latest developments and emerging problems in education by eminent academicians and scholars may be organised.

5. *Dissemination*

SCERT's/SIE's bring out reports of research studies, news letters, journals/magazines, annual reports, etc. They also disseminate important data, information, significant research findings through their news letters/magazines and annual reports to the concerned institutions.

6. *Linkage of SCERT with other Institutions*

In the field of elementary education the Directorate of Education, Department of Adult and non-formal education and DIET's are the main Institutions with which the SCERT should have close relations and coordination.

In the area of pre-school education SCERT is expected to prepare guidelines for organising the activities at the child play centres, Anganwadis, Balwadis, etc. Integrated Child Development services (ICDS) run by the Social Welfare Department mainly dealt with health and nutrition components.

DIET: Role and Functions

Here we discussed the role and functions of District Institute of Education and Training (DIET) as derived from NPE (1986) and POA (1992).

Elementary education is very crucial for developing human resource which in turn promotes the growth of economy. One of the road block, which impedes our march towards the goal is high drop out rate at elementary level.

The NPE (1986) envisaged setting up the DIET's in the country with a view to improving the quality of elementary education. It was envisaged the DIET's would provide pre-service as well as inservice education to all the elementary teachers in the district.

The functioning of a DIET involves providing academic and resource support to achieve Universalisation of Elementary Education (UEE) and improve quality of elementary education, non-formal education and adult education and strengthening elementary teacher training, both pre-service and in-service.

The DIET has the following major functions to perform:

1. Conducting Training.
2. Providing academic and resource support to the elementary and adult education system in the district.
3. Conducting action research and experimentation to deal with specific problems relating to universal elementary and adult education.

DIET: Its Organisational Structure

As per the guidelines of MHRD, a DIET would have the following seven academic branches.

1. *Pre-Service Teacher Education (PSTE) Branch*: This Branch is to organise a regular full time two years teacher's training programme for 50 students.

2. *In-service Field Interaction and Innovations Coordination (FIC) Branch:* DIET will regularly organise in-service teacher orientation programmes for teacher to equip them to meet the changing demands of the profession.

3. *Work Experience (WE) Branch*: This branch identified locally relevant work experience areas and works for their inclusion in the curriculum of elementary schools.

4. *Educational Technology (ET) Branch:* The primary functions of this branch are to:

   (a) equip the institute with a variety of educational gadgets for enriching the quality of education and teacher training,
   (b) develop different programmes of media intervention as input for quality schooling: and,
   (c) prepare teaching/learning material for pre-service and in-service teacher training and non-formal education and Adult Education workers.

5. *Planning and Management (P & M) Branch*: This unit of DIET plays the role of a nodal agency for assessing, planning, advising and meeting over all education needs and aspirations of the district covering primary education.

6. *Curriculum, Material Development and Evaluation (CMDE) Branch:* The role and responsibility of the branch is to develop curriculum and learning materials for elementary education, teacher education, adult education and non-formal education.

7. *District Resource Unit (DRU):* Primary responsibility of this unit is to assist in planning, coordinating and organising programmes for adult and non-formal education personnel on a continuing basis.

DIET: Measures to Improve Functioning

1. The DIET may establish a close cooperation and continuing dialogue with the field to fully involve local expertise and

local resources for overall educational development of the district.

2. The DIET being a nodal agency in the district, may develop a long term calendar of its developmental activities and educational programmes clearly spelt out on a frequent occasions.
3. The DIET may undertake microplanning, field studies and adopt area specific approach for identifying and tackling specific problems through action research, experimentation and other suitable measures.
4. The DIET may promote innovations in methodology of teaching, revision of curriculum, textbooks and other teaching materials.
5. The DIET may devise strategies for realising minimum levels of learning by elementary school children and also organise mass literary programmes with peoples participation.
6. The DIET should strive to ensure full involvement of the community in the educational development of the district.
7. The DIET should develop a rich and ever-growing library having sufficient resources.
8. The DIET should try to exploit media intervention both print and visual.

Let's concluding, the concept of grass root planning and development has been gaining ground in the country for quite a while. The getting up of institutions like the DIETs at the District Level seems to be a positive step in this direction.

REFERENCES

1. Govt. of India, *Education and National Development the Report of Education Commission*, New Delhi: Manager of Publications, 1966. pp. 149-151.
2. Government of India, *District Institute of Education and Training: Guidelines*, MHRD, New Delhi, 1989.
3. Government of India, *National Policy on Education*, MHRD, New Delhi, 1986.

16

Administration of Pre-School and Elementary Institutions

Educational administration is a comprehensive effort to direct, guide and integrate associating human strivings which are focused towards some specific ends or aims.

Educational Administration is also a comprehensive effort intended to achieve some specific, educational objectives and it deals with the educational practices, whereas educational philosophy sets the goals, educational psychology explains the principles, educational administration tells the how of educational objectives and principles.

It in fact, is the dynamic side of education.

Educational administration deals with educational institutions-right from the schools and colleges to the secretariat. It is concerned with both human and material resources.

The human elements include:

- Children
- Parents
- Teachers
- Other employees in general University or Board of Education at Local, State and National levels of Government.

Material Side

- Money
- Building and grounds
- Equipment and Instructional supplies

Beyond these two elements are Idea-Laws and regulations, community needs and so on.

The integration of these 'parts' into a 'whole' is educational administration. Kandel, says the purpose of Educational Administration is to bring pupils and teachers under such conditions as well more successfully promote the end of education.

Sir Graham Balfour writes very aptly the purpose of educational administration is to enable the right people to receive the right education from the right teacher, at a cost within the means of the state, which will enable pupils to profit by their learning.

How of Educational Administration: The Process

Educational Administration has the following components:

1. Fore casting
2. Decision Making
3. Planning
4. Organisation
5. Direction or Motivation
6. Control
7. Coordination
8. Evaluation
9. Recording and Reporting

Administration and Organisation

These two terms are not antagonistic but are two distinct phases of the one process of purpose achievement through from any institution or enterprise are not to be expected.

Organisation is concerned with the arrangement and rearrangement of equipment, material, apparatus and persons, the administrator is to operate and manage the things so organised.

So administration and organisation must run side by side on parallel lines to help each and supplement the efforts of one another.

Scope of School Administration

The following may be consider as necessary components of School Administration.

1. Providing the human equipment- headmaster, teaching, staff, ministerial staff and menial staff.
2. Providing the material equipment such as building, furniture, farms, laboratory, library, museum, art gallery, etc.
3. Preparing the curriculum for the different classes.
4. Organisation of a systematic co-curricular programme.
5. Preparing timetable.
6. Maintaining discipline.
7. Organisation of library, museum, hostel, etc.
8. Organisation of exhibition and museum.
9. Organisation of health and physical education.
10. Organisation of guidance service.
11. Maintaining school records.
12. Providing various auxiliary services like mid-day meals, school uniform, textbooks, etc.
13. Coordinating the work of home, school and community.
14. Supervision of school work.
15. Evaluation of pupil achievement.
16. Financing and budgeting.
17. Cooperating with departmental authorities and implementing the orders of the higher educational authorities.

Characteristics of Successful School Administration

There are some essential features in a good school administration.

1. *Flexibility*

The administration should be dynamic, not static. It should provide enough scope for addition and alterations. The rules and regulations should act as a means to an end not an end in themselves.

The flexibility does not mean that the administration should be in a fluid condition without any specific norm or standard rules and regulations, creating confusion and chaos at every step. What is meant is a proper balance between rigidity and elasticity.

2. *Practicability*

The school administration must not be a bundle of theoretical principles, but must provide practical measures to achieve the desired objectives. Whatever objectives is decided it must be achievable and practical to avoid frustration.

3. ***Conformity to the School and Political Philosophy of the Country***

There must be close communication between school administration and the social and political philosophy of the country. It must adjust itself to the impact of new ideals, new patterns and new norms of the society. In an autocratic country, educational theory and practice will have be different from that of a democratic country because education is one of the means to achieve social and political objectives.

American education is decentralised and democratised whereas Chinese education is characterised by regimentation due to political philosophies of the respective countries. In India, school administration has to be democratic because of political democracy in the country.

Efficiency

Maximum efficiency. This will be possible when men and material resources are properly utilised right man at the right time and right place. Right work at right time, every activity and project is well planned and well executed.

Successful Achievement of Desired Objectives

E.g.: Healthy school living, development of good physical, social, moral, intellectual and aesthetic qualities and healthy democratic living.

School administration must facilitate education. It exerts for the pupils and its efficiency has to be measured by the extent to which it constitutes to teaching and learning.

Principles of Democratic School Administration

India happens to be the largest democracy in the world. To make democracy successful, we have to revitalise and recharge our school to the full. School will be able to add tempo to the struggling democracy if the following principles are taken into consideration while administering them.

1. *Democratic Philosophy of Education*

Dr. Paul H. Appleby, in his Report in India Administration has emphasised the need for a philosophical but simple theory for administration for a country which is determined to create a welfare state. If a philosophy is necessary for general administration, it is all the more so for educational administration which is seeking to fashion a new pattern of education suited to the needs and aspiration of modern India.

In an educational institution in a democracy, the administrator is not a small dictator, but a friend and guide; he consults his colleagues, honours their opinions, confer with them in the staff meeting, meets them informally in gatherings and clubs he is one among the equals. He recognises the work of each individual child, finds out his potentialities and gives him help and guidance according to his requirements. Thus, the total administration becomes a joint show of the Headmaster, teacher and pupils. Everybody has a clear conscious and realisation of the purpose of democratic philosophy with which the school is administered.

Freedom

Enough freedom should be given to all to exercise their power and talents. The power of critical thinking, an important requisite of democracy, can only be cultivated by individuals in an atmosphere of freedom.

Students Centred

The purpose of all educational endeavour is the welfare of the student. This flesh and blood should never be lost sight of in the midst of facts, figures and files. Enough opportunities must be provided for the whole development of the students. Whatever is done in the school should be of the students, by the students and for the students.

The Administration Must be Flexible Adaptable and Stable

It must hold fast to the good, charge what requires changing and be fertile in considering individual differences in all personalities involved.

Democracy can only become real though its education institutions which will teach its children the democratic way of life. There must pervade an atmosphere of justice, freedom and cooperation in the educational institution. Only then good training in leadership and fellowship can be given.

Practical Measures for Democratic School Administration

1. *Staff Council*

The aim of staff council should be to plan all important matters of the school. The staff council may be further split up into committees to plan and execute specific tasks. Meetings of the staff council should be held frequently to discuss all urgent issues.

2. *Students Council*

A students council consisting of secretaries for different houses association and clubs should from a student's council with the aim of giving the students training in self-government. The student's council can be guided and assisted by a staff advisor.

3. *Staff Meetings*

Meeting of the staff should be called fortnightly to discuss the different matters and the staff should have an idea that whatever has been dealing upon is mainly their work.

Special Committee of Pupils

In addition to the student council, special committees should be formed duly elected by the pupils to carry out specific duties and organise special activities for maintaining disciplines, organising debates, dramas, exhibitions, flower shows, literary societies, music concerts, etc.

Social Service Squads

Such type of squads can render service in the form of laying roads, arranging committee functions, cleanliness campaigns in the neighbourhood, literary campaigns, helping the sick, looking after the families of the jawans, collection of national defence fund, etc.

REFERENCES

1. Aggarwal, J.C. (2003). *Development and Planning of Modern Education*. New Delhi: Vikas Publishing House (P.) Ltd.

2. Murty, S.K. (1992). *Contemporary Problems and Current Trends in Education*. Ludhiana: Parkash Brothers.
3. Chaube, S.P. & Chaube, A. (1987). *Foundations of Education*. New Delhi: Vikas Publishing House (P.) Ltd.
4. Ganta, R. and Dash, B.N. (2005). *Foundations of Education*. Hyderabad: Neelkamal Publishers (P) Ltd.
5. Taneja, R.P. (2000). *Dictionary of Education*. Anmol Publishing Ltd.

17

Elementary Education in India Since Independence

Universalisation of Elementary Education (UEE) has been accepted as a national goal in India since Independence. The founding fathers of our Constitution recognised UEE as a crucial input for nation building. The Directive Principles of State Policy envisage that the state shall endeavour to provide free and compulsory education for children up to 14 years of age within a period of 10 years. The National Education Policies so far have reiterated the constitutional directive. The National Policy on Education 1986 (as revised in 1992) resolves to provide free and compulsory education of satisfactory quality to all children up to 14 years of age before the commencement of the twenty first century.

The colonial regime prior to our Independence in 1947 established a system of education that had limited access and denied mass education. It gave greater emphasis on conformism to socio-political and economic systems obtaining in the country in those times. Macaulay explicitly stated that the objective of the education system was to create a new breed of Indians as similar to Europeans as possible. It was on account of this that the Indian National Movement developed a strong critique of the British System that only imparted 'learning skills' and not 'life skills' and that did not respect Indian traditions. The national movement also expressed the global sentiment of education for all and Gopal Krishna Gokhale's Compulsory Education Bill reflected the spirit of India's freedom movement.

The imperatives of the colonial education policy promoted alternatives, notable being Mahatma Gandhi's "education for life" and Rabindra Nath Tagore's approach of education for self-development, reflected through Shantiniketan. Dr. Zakir Hussain's thrust on 'Nayee Taleem' was also based on Gandhiji's philosophy of education for life. Gandhiji's emphasis on "Swawalamban" sprang from his belief that the State was not the best agency to promote education. He believed that education is a process of empowerment. It integrates physical, mental and emotional development. He stressed that education must promote respect for manual labour rather than abhorrence for it.

Fresh Approach

The favour for freedom and patriotism to achieve "swawalamban", made our leaders search for an alternative approach to elementary education. Article 41 and 45 of the Constitution enunciating the Directive Principles of State Policy on education provided the basis for the new approach. 14 States and 4 Union Territories enacted Legislation for free and compulsory primary education. All States have exempted children from tuition fee up to upper primary classes. However, compulsion has not been enforced due to socio-economic and political considerations.

Expansion and Growth

The thrust of the Central and State Governments in universalising elementary education so far has been on three aspects namely, universal access, universal retention and universal achievement. Concerted efforts made in these areas have resulted in significant expansion of elementary education in the country. The number of primary schools has increased from 2.10 lakh in 1950-51 to 5.90 lakh and number of upper primary schools from 13,000 to 1.71 lakh respectively in 1995-96. During this period, Gross Enrolment Ratio (GER) at primary levels has increased from 43 per cent in 1950-51 to 104 per cent in 1995-96. 95 per cent of the rural population in the country has a primary school within 1 kilometre and 85 per cent an upper primary school within a distance of 3 kilometres. With 15 Crore children enrolled and 30 lakh teachers, we have one of the largest elementary education systems in the world. The proportion of girls in classes I-VIII as also women teachers has increased steadily.

Results of Efforts Towards UEE

	No. of Institutions (in lakhs)	
	1950-51	*1995-96*
Primary Schools: Classes I-V	2.10	5.90
Upper Primary Schools: Classes VI-VIII	0.13	1.71
Total	**2.23**	**7.61**
	No. of Teachers (in lakhs)	
Primary Schools: Classes I-V	5.38	17.40
Upper Primary Schools: Classes VI-VIII	0.36	11.65
Total	**6.24**	**29.05**

	Gross Enrolment	
	1950-51	*1995-96*
Primary Stage		
Total Enrolment (in million)	19.2	109.73
Gross Enrolment Ratio percentage	43.1	104.30
Upper Primary Stage		
Total Enrolment (in million)	3.1	41.01
Gross Enrolment Ratio percentage	12.0	67.20

Quality Improvement

The quality of elementary education has been one of the major concerns right from 1950s. The National Policy on Education, 1986 brought to the forefront the need for quality improvement in terms of learning achievement of children. As a result, greater efforts have been made to impart competency-based learning, particularly from 1990 when the Minimum Levels of Learning (MLLs) were introduced. A clear shift from teacher dominated teaching to a child centred approach has been observed in most states. Integrated Textbooks, which include workbooks, are replacing traditional books. A large number of teaching, learning and reading materials have been developed, with active participation of teachers and NGOs. Efforts are continuing to promote competency based learning both at primary and upper primary levels by re-orienting and training teachers. Results so far have been encouraging.

Policy and Planning

The period after Independence saw a linear expansion of the elementary education system through allocation of additional resources. It was in 1964 that the Central Government recognised the need to take a holistic view of education and appointed the Education Commission (1964-66). The Commission was entrusted with the task of evolving a national system of education. It recommended a radical transformation in the prevailing education system and highlighted the need for the "common school approach" to promote equity and social justice. The first National Policy on Education, 1968 recommended free and compulsory elementary education and equalisation of educational opportunities especially for girls and children belonging to SCs and STs. The National Policy on Education 1986 and its Programme of Action, (1992) was enunciated on the basis of a detailed review of the country's educational performance. The policy resolves to achieve UEE by 2000 AD.

The plan allocations for elementary education have increased steadily, though still not adequate to fulfils the constitutional commitments. Fifty years of freedom have seen higher levels of spending by the Central and State Governments to provide quality of education for all. Better school infrastructure, more and better-paid school teachers, timely availability of subsidised or free text-books in regional languages, provision of scholarships, uniforms and mid day meals have all received attention of state governments who are the main providers of elementary education. The Central Government increased its allocations for elementary education after 1976 when education became a concurrent subject. These allocations were aimed at providing additional funds to resource poor states on the basis of the principle of equalisation and for quality improvement.

The period following the adoption of National Policy on Education (NPE), 1986 saw the introduction of a number of centrally sponsored schemes to cater to the specific needs of the elementary education sector. These included Operation Blackboard (1987) to improve school environment, enhance retention and learning achievement of children by providing minimum essential facilities in all primary schools; restructuring and strengthening of Teacher

Education (1987) to upgrade pedagogical skills of teachers through establishment of dedicated teacher training institutes at District level (DIETS); Non-formal Education Programme (1987) to provide alternative education facilities for girls, working children and children in far flung areas; Minimum Levels of Learning (1990) to improve learning achievements of children; and the National Programme of Nutritional Support to Primary Education, commonly known as Mid-day Meal Scheme, to provide nutritional support to children in primary classes.

Plan expenditure on elementary education has increased to nearly 50 per cent of Central expenditure on Education. States continue to discharge the main responsibility for management, expansion and maintenance of schools. Since there is considerable variation in their fiscal capacity to do so, there is need for targeted interventions to improve primary education in such states.

External Assistance

Following the World Conference for Education for All (EFA) in Jomtien (Thailand) in March 1990 there is a greater commitment and willingness on the part of multilateral and bilateral aid agencies to invest in primary education in developing countries. A major internationally assisted programme namely District Primary Education Programme (DPEP) was launched in 1992 with assistance from World Bank and European Union. The programme adopts a holistic approach to promote primary education through decentralised planning and integrated programming at district level. The programme has been extended to 149 districts in 14 States in 1997. The Lok Jumbish and Shiksha Karmi Projects are two other successful internationally assisted projects. Lok Jumbish, meaning a people's movement for UEE, has a holistic understanding about the problem of UEE and is implemented by establishing an interface between the local community, the teaching profession, the educational administration and the learners. The Shiksha Karmi Project envisages a paradigm shift in delivery of primary education. Inspired by the concept of barefoot teachers, the project has effectively responded to the problem of teacher absenteeism in the remote and inaccessible areas of Rajasthan.

Internationally assisted projects for basic education have focused attention on decentralisation, people's participation, construction of school buildings, development of innovative teaching learning materials, participative teacher training, enhancement of institutional capacities and improvement in learning levels. The overall strategy and approach of these projects gives priority to low literacy areas, girls and disadvantaged sections of society.

Decentralisation and Community Mobilisation

The process of decentralisation has been an encouraging feature of our efforts to universalise elementary education. NPE, 1986 visualises direct community involvement in the form of Village Education Committees (VECs) for management of elementary education. The POA, 1992 emphasised micro-planning as a process of designing a family-wise and child-wise plan of education by which every child regularly attends a school or a NFE centre, continues his or her education at a place suitable to him/her and completes at least eight years of schooling or its equivalent at the NFE centre.

The Seventy-third and Seventy-fourth Constitutional Amendments have hastened the process of community management of elementary schools. These amendments have created a congenial ambience for the Panchayat Raj Institutions (PRIs) to play a more dynamic role. These institutions now provide a greater voice to women, scheduled castes and scheduled tribes. Increasingly PRIs and VECs are becoming involved in social mobilisation, planning and supervision for UEE. The introduction of micro-planning and school mapping have brought the school closer to the community while sensitising people to issues and problems in their local schools.

Recent trends in community participation indicate a greater thrust on empowerment of communities. Mobilising the communities to take responsibility to ensure quality education for every child is the core strategy of several innovative initiatives in elementary education including DPEP, LJP, SKP and BEP. Genuine community involvement is the key factor for the success of LJP and SKP in Rajasthan. LJP has had a positive effect on the empowerment of locally elected people, especially women at village level who are often active members of the LJ core teams and Mahila Samoohs. The VECs, carefully formed and trained through environmental building activities in the LJ, are actively involved in school matters. SKP has constituted VECs in 2000 villages to promote community involvement in primary education and encourage village level planning. DPEP is making useful investments in orientation and training of VEC members. An important role of the VEC is to mobilise resources for maintenance, repair and construction of school buildings. The VECs also help in determining the school calendar and school timings in consultation with the local community.

Partnership with NGOs

NGOs are emerging as important partners in efforts of the Central and State Governments towards UEE. They have been instrumental in mobilising social support for UEE, development of socially relevant curriculum, contextual teaching learning materials, innovative teacher training, pedagogic renewal, review and evaluation of educational experiments, action research for UEE, and designing of alternative education programmes. The participation of NGOs together with community support has helped to improve the physical conditions and environment of elementary schools as well as promotion of education for girls and children belonging to SCs and STs and working children. As of now, nearly 750 NGOs are supplementing the Governmental efforts towards UEE by rendering cooperation and resource support to Non-formal Education with assistance from the Government.

Future Challenges

The country has undoubtedly been successful in evolving a national structure for elementary education in the last fifty years. Primary education is now provided in the mother tongue or regional language in all the States and UTs. There has been substantial increase in access to elementary education, with reduced class, caste and sectional disparities. First generation learners, girls and the under privileged sections of society have been provided with unique opportunities for vertical mobility. Literacy standards have substantially improved across all the States and UTs. National Literacy rate has increased from 15 per cent in 1951 to 52 per cent in 1991. An impressive academic support system has been built up at national and state level through NCERT, NIEPA, NCTE, SCERTs, CIEMATs, DIETs, BRCs, and CRCs to provide technical support and guidance to the elementary education system.

Despite substantial achievements, the task of UEE is far from complete. Schools and enrolments have certainly increased but so have the number of out of school children. The country today has one of the largest illiterate populations in the world. Caste, gender, class and regional disparities in UEE though reduced, are still glaring and persistent. While the demand for quality education is showing perceptible increase because of improved awareness and social mobilisation through organised efforts such as TLCs and PLCs, supply is generally inadequate. The educational administration in most states and UTs is yet to effectively tackle endemic problems concerning shortage of teachers, teacher absenteeism, inadequate and improperly designed school buildings, lack of teaching learning equipment, need based teacher training, and a curriculum related to real life requirements. Teachers' esteem in a society that worshipped Gurus is low. They are called upon to do variety of non-teaching jobs, leaving little time for teacher-pupil interaction. Teacher education, considered crucial to improve quality of education, has not made the vital difference in the classroom.

A traditional style of administration and the tendency for centralisation is impeding genuine people's participation and effective partnership with NGOs. Lack of transparency and rigid procedures have not facilitated confidence building measures necessary for empowerment of women and the poor

Imperative in these shortfalls is the need to consolidate the gains, design specifically targeted programmes to reach the unreached, improve quality of education making it contextually relevant and related to real life, and make UEE a social movement. We need to redouble our efforts in promoting education for girls, SCs and STs and minorities. Research in educational planning, management and training should be given greater attention in our endeavour to improve learning achievement of children in schools.

The recent measures initiated by the Government, namely DPEP, Mid-day Meal Programme and the proposal for NEEM, the National Programme Media advocacy and Publicity for UEE and the Joint GOI-UN System Education Programme are expected to address some of these challenges more effectively. The proposed National Elementary Education Mission should evolve strategies for reaching the unreached and achieving the goal of UEE within a given time-frame in a systematic, sustained and integrated manner by involving all segments of civil society in this national endeavour. The resolve of the Government to make elementary education a fundamental right of all children of 6-14 years is expected to spur the government and non-government sectors to take necessary measures to achieve UEE. It is a demonstration of political will and administrative resolve to achieve UEE and eradicate illiteracy. Efforts of the Government to mobilise resources for education to the extent of 6 per cent of GDP will also help in hastening the process of universalising elementary education.

Undeniably, we face a gigantic challenge to achieve UEE. Nevertheless, in the last fifty years we have expanded our base and built many assets to complete the unfinished task in the foreseeable future. We have a strong policy framework, significant political and administrative commitment and a national desire for UEE.

It is hoped that with a clear vision, firm will, higher investments, greater dedication, rapid decentralisation and increased people's participation, we would be able to fulfil our goal of providing satisfactory quality of education to all children in the country within the next decade.

REFERENCE

1. Abhimanyu Singh, *Fifty Years of Elementary Education*, Department of Education, Government of India.

18

Tenth Five Year Plan (2002-2007) and Elementary Education

Education is a critical input in human resource development and is essential for the country's economic growth. Though the major indicators of socio-economic development viz., the growth rate of the economy, birth rate, death rate, infant mortality rate (IMR) and literacy rate, are all interconnected, the literacy rate has been the major determinant of the rise or fall in the other indicators. There is enough evidence even in India to show that a high literacy rate, especially in the case of women, correlates with low birth rate, low IMR and increase in the rate of life expectancy. The recognition of this fact has created awareness on the need to focus upon literacy and elementary education programmes, not simply as a matter of social justice but more to foster economic growth, social well-being and social stability.

Review of Past Performance

Article 45 of the Constitution stipulates that the 'State shall endeavour to provide, within a period of 10 years from the commencement of the Constitution, for free and compulsory education for all children until they complete the age of 14 years.' However, the task of providing basic education for all, with concrete plans of action, gained greater momentum only after the National Policy of Education (NPE), 1986 (revised in 1992). With the World Declaration on Education for All (EFA) adopted in Jomtein in 1990, basic education in all its facets (Early Child Care Education (ECCE), elementary education, education for adolescents, adult education, gender equality and quality improvement) has been the focus of international attention. These international developments, together with several positive developments within the country, brought the need for recognising basic education as a fundamental right of every citizen to the centre stage. With the launching of the National Policy on Education in 1986, the Government initiated a move to start a number of missions. The National Literacy Mission, started in 1988, was one such mission. It had the following aims:

- increase motivation, which is the central issue in literacy;
- secure participation by creating a positive environment and through mass mobilisation;
- increase the involvement of voluntary agencies and enhance the quality of existing programmes with improved techno-pedagogic inputs;
- launch a mass movement for expanding the Mass Functional Literacy Programme (MFLP), hitherto confined to university, college and secondary/higher secondary schools, to include different sections of society;
- ensure the availability of quality learning materials, aligned to mission goals;
- universalise the outreach of literacy learning facilities to all parts of the country by 1990; and
- establish a Mission Management System for monitoring and for corrective action.

The central government, in partnership with state governments, has initiated a number of programmes to fulfil the Constitutional obligationand national aspirations.

Growth of Literacy

Over the decades, literacy rates have shown substantial improvement. The total literacy rate, which was only 16.67 per cent in 1951 rose to 52.21 per cent in 1991. The provisional results of the 2001 Census indicate that the literacy rate has gone up to 65.37 per cent - 75.85 per cent for males and 54.16 per cent for females. For the first time, the number of illiterates has, in absolute terms, decreased by 31.9 million. The number of literates, on the other hand, has increased by 203.6 million between 1991 and 2001. During the period, the female literacy rate increased by 14.87 per cent as against 11.72 per cent in the case of males, thus reducing the male-female literacy gap to 21.7 per cent from 24.84 per cent in 1991. All states have, without exception, registered an increase in literacy rates of both males and females during the last decade. Table 18.1 gives the literacy rates over the decades:

Table–18.1
Literacy Rate 1951-2001

	Male	*Female*	*Total*
1951	24.95	7.93	16.67
1961	34.44	12.95	24.02
1971	39.45	18.69	29.45
1981	64.13	39.29	52.21
2001 (provisional)	75.85	54.16	65.37

Enrolment Trends

Enrolment at the primary level (grades I to V) increased from 19.16 million in 1950-51 to 113.61 million in 1999-2000. In comparison, the growth in enrolment at the upper primary level (grades VI to VIII) has been much more impressive, although it is still not adequate to attain the Constitutional goal of universal enrolment of children up to the age of 14. From 3.12 million in 1950-51, enrolment at the upper primary level increased to 42.06 million in 1999-2000, indicating a 13.5 times increase as against six times at the primary level. The percentage share of girls in total enrolment, both at the primary and upper primary levels, has increased consistently between 1950-51 (28.1 per cent) and 1999-2000 (43.6 per cent). However, girls' share in total enrolment at the upper primary level (40.4 per cent) continues to be lower than their share at the primary level in 1999-2000.

Enrolment Ratios

The Gross Enrolment Ratio (GER) at the primary and upper primary levels improved significantly between 1950-51 and 1999-2000, from 42.6 to 94.9 in the case of primary levels and from 12.7 to 58.79 for upper primary levels. The gap between boys and girls in GER at the primary and upper primary levels has declined significantly from 28.5 and 29.6 percentage points respectively in 1990-91 to 19 and 18 in 1999-2000.

The Net Enrolment Ratios (NER), obtained by subtracting the number of underage and overage children enrolled in grades I-V and VI-VIII, were significantly lower than GER in the case of both boys and girls. The NER for boys and girls was 78 per cent and 64 per cent respectively at the primary level in 1997-98. The overall NER at the primary level was 71 per cent, which suggests that at least 29 per cent of children in the 6-10 age group continued to remain out of school in 1997-98. Educationally backward states, and, within them, backward districts, have lower NER than the all-India average.

Educational Facilities

The availability of schooling facilities is measured by a set of indicators concerning access. Existing norms stipulate that a habitation (cluster of households) is entitled to have a primary school, if it has a population of 300 and more and has no school within a distance of 1 km. Upper primary schools are to be located at a distance of 3 km from habitations with a population of 500 and more. These norms are often relaxed in case of hilly and tribal areas, difficult terrains and border districts.

During the period 1950-51 to 1999-2000, the number of primary schools has increased by more than three times from 2,10,000 in 1950-51 to 6,42,000 in 1999-2000 whereas the number of upper primary schools increased by about 15 times from 13,600 in 1950-51 to 1,98,000 in 1999-2000. The ratio of upper primary school to primary schools came down from 1:15 in 1950-51 to 1:3.2 in 1999-2000.

The total number of teachers increased from 6,24,000 in 1950-51 to 3.2 million in 1999-2000, an increase of more than five times. The number of female teachers increased from 95,000 in 1950-51 to 11,52,000 in 1999-2000, an increase of more than 12 times. The percentage of female teachers to total teachers, which was 15.2 per cent at the primary level and 15.1 per cent at upper primary level in 1950-51 has increased to 35.6 and 36.1 per cent respectively in 1999-2000. However, the teacher-pupil ratio (TPR) has worsened over the years. During 1950-51, the TPR in primary schools was 1:24, and 1:20 in middle schools. In 1999-2000, this ratio has increased to 1:43 in primary schools and 1:38 in upper primary schools.

Despite an increase in the number of habitations and population, the coverage of both primary and upper primary schools, in line with the norms, has increased significantly. Of the one million rural habitations in the country, 5,28,000 had a primary school within the habitation itself in 1993-94. About 83.4 per cent habitations had a primary school/section within a 1 km distance. Presently, about 1,00,000 habitations remain unserved as per prescribed norms. The alternative and innovative programme envisages opening of non-formal education (NFE) centres in habitations where opening of a full-fledged school is not economically feasible or academically viable. Over a period of time, infrastructure and other facilities in schools have also improved significantly although a large number of primary and upper primary schools continue to suffer from deficiencies, making it difficult for them to function smoothly and preventing them from providing optimal conditions for teaching and learning.

REVIEW OF NINTH PLAN

The Ninth Plan regarded education as the most crucial investment in human development. The Prime Minister's Special Action Plan gave emphasis to the total eradication of illiteracy, equal access to and opportunity of education up to the school-leaving stage, improvement in the quality of education at all levels, and the need for expansion and improvement of infrastructural facilities. The thrust areas in the Ninth Plan included UEE, full adult literacy, raising the quality of education at all levels and improving learner achievement. The Plan also emphasised improvement of the educational status of disadvantaged groups, including scheduled castes (SC) and scheduled tribes (ST), girls and disabled children and the removal of regional disparities. In addition, it stressed the vocationalisation of education, revision of the curriculum to meet emerging challenges in information technology and support for development of centres of excellence at the tertiary level.

Elementary education was given the highest priority in sub-sectoral allocations within the education sector, indicating a strong reiteration of the country's resolve to achieve the goal of EFA during the Plan period. The goal was sought to be achieved through several measures, which included:

- Amendment of the Constitution to make elementary education a fundamental right;
- decentralisation of planning, supervision and management of education through local bodies at the district, block and village levels;
- social mobilisation of local communities for adult literacy through campaigns and for promotion of primary education;
- convergence of different schemes for UEE;
- stronger partnership with non-governmental organisations (NGOs) and voluntary organisations;
- advocacy and media campaign for UEE;
- provision of opportunities for non-formal and alternative education for out-of-school children in the most backward areas and for unreached segments of the population in response to local needs and demands; and
- universal participation and retention rather than universal enrolment. The goal of UEE was enlarged to include provision of education of a satisfactory quality to all children.

Achievements of Ninth Plan

As a result of the various intervention strategies, the progress in terms of access was impressive. According to the Sixth All-India Education Survey (1993), 94 per cent of the rural population living in 8.84 lakh habitations now has a school within a walking distance of 1 km and 85 per cent have an upper primary school within a walking distance of 3 km. The situation has improved significantly thereafter. During the first three years of the Ninth Plan (1997-2000), over 43,000 new schools were opened and 1,30,000 new teachers recruited at the primary level, while more than 21,000 new schools and 1,02,000 teachers added in the upper primary schools. The GER at the primary level increased from 90.6 per cent in 1996-97 to 94.9 per cent in 1999-2000, while it declined from 62.4 per cent to 58.8 per cent at the upper primary level during the same period. The dropout rate at the primary level declined from 42.4 per cent in 1998-99 to 40.3 per cent in 1999-2000, while in the upper primary stage it fell from 56.8 per cent to 54.5 per cent.

Despite the significant improvement in access to elementary education in the Ninth Plan, the achievement is short of target as the Plan had envisaged additional enrolment of 25 million children in the primary stage and 16 million children in the upper primary stage. It had also targeted the construction of 75,000 school buildings/additional classrooms at the elementary stage and the appointment of 2,36,000 teachers at the primary level and 1,75,000 teachers at the upper primary level.

PROGRAMMES/SCHEMES

Operation Blackboard

The Operation Blackboard scheme, started in 1987-88, which aimed at improving the classroom environment by providing infrastructural facilities, additional teachers and teaching-learning material to primary schools and by provision of a third teacher to schools where enrolment exceeded 100, has been extended to upper primary schools. A total of 5,23,000 primary schools and 1,27,000 upper primary schools have been provided funds for the development of academic infrastructure (teaching-learning material). Besides, 1,50,000 posts of additional teachers for single teacher primary schools, 76,000 posts of additional teachers at the upper primary stage and 83,000 posts of third teachers have been sanctioned so far.

Restructuring and Reorganisation of Teacher Education

The scheme of Restructuring and Reorganisation of Teacher Education, started in 1987, aims to strengthen the institutional base of teacher training by taking up special programmes for training of teachers in specified areas and other non-institutional training programmes. Other objectives of the scheme are: setting up District Institutes of Education and Training (DIETs) to provide academic and resource support to elementary school teachers and non-formal and adult education instructors; and establishment of Colleges of Teacher Education (CTEs) and Institutes of Advanced Studies in Education (IASEs) for preservice and in-service training for secondary school teachers. The scheme also envisages strengthening State Councils of Educational Research and Training (SCERT); orienting teachers in the use of Operation Blackboard material; and implementation of the Minimum Levels of Learning (MLL) strategy.

Under this scheme, 471 DIETs, 86 CTEs, 38 IASEs have been sanctioned so far. More than 1.9 million teachers have been trained under the Special Orientation Programme of School Teachers in the use of Operation Blackboard material and implementation of the

MLL strategy. The scheme has recently been revamped with greater thrust on improving the quality of teacher training institutions in partnership with states. The revised scheme provides for more assistance to states; memorandums of understanding (MoU) with states to improve the efficiency of key resource institutes; widening the scope of the Special Orientation Programme for school teachers; and enhancing the capacities of existing personnel for the management of teacher education programmes.

District Primary Education Programme (DPEP)

The District Primary Education Programme (DPEP), launched in 1994, is assisted by the World Bank, European Commission, Department for International Development (DFID) of the United Kingdom, the Netherlands and the United Nations International Children's Emergency Fund (UNICEF). It aims at operationalising the strategies for achieving UPE/UEE through district-specific planning and disaggregated target setting in low female literacy districts and builds on the successful Total Literacy Campaign (TLC) which has created a favourable climate for universalisation. Eightyfive per cent of the funds for the project come from external agencies through the central budget and the remaining 15 per cent is given by the concerned state governments. The programme components include construction of classrooms and new schools, opening of the non-formal/alternative schooling centres, appointment of new teachers, and setting up of early childhood education (ECE) centres, strengthening of SCERTs and DIETs, and setting up of block resource centres/cluster resource centres. It also comprises teacher training, interventions, development of teaching-learning material, research and a thrust on education of girls, SC/ST, etc. A new initiative of providing integrated education to disabled children and distance education for teacher training has also been incorporated in the DPEP scheme.

Under DPEP, 21,000 new formal schools and over 67,000 new alternative schools have been opened, covering 2.5 million children, and 20,000 bridge courses conducted. The programme has set up over 10,000 ECE centres and strengthened more than 50,000 pre-primary centres of anganwadis. DPEP has provided training to over three million community members and about one million teachers. About 27,700 school buildings, 37,000 classrooms and 11,100 resource centres have been completed or are in progress in DPEP districts. The programme now covers about 50 per cent of the children in the primary stage in over 271 districts in 18 states.

Shiksha Karmi Project and Lok Jumbish Project in Rajasthan

Two externally-aided projects for basic education are the Shiksha Karmi and Lok Jumbish projects in Rajasthan. Both are innovative projects aimed at the universalisation of elementary education together with a qualitative improvement in remote and socially backward villages with a primary focus on gender. The projects address some of the major obstacles in achieving UEE, namely, teacher absenteeism, high dropout rate, working children, uninteresting teaching methods, lack of contextual learning materials, low motivation and competence of teachers, a centralised and inflexible approach, etc. There is a special emphasis on community participation in these projects. The Village Education Committees (VECs) have contributed a great deal to the improvement of the school environment, augmentation of infrastructure and facilities, larger enrolment of children through school mapping and micro-planning in the Shiksha Karmi schools. The Shiksha Karmi project covers 2,708 villages in 147 blocks spread over 31 districts and has been responsible for a seven-fold increase in the enrolment of children in schools taken over by the project.

The Lok Jumbish project has been able to set up innovative management structures incorporating the principles of decentralisation and delegation of authority as well as building partnerships with local communities and the voluntary sector. The project has also made a positive contribution to quality improvement through the development of improved MLL-based textbooks for Classes I-IV, which are also being used in all schools in Rajasthan. It has conducted school mapping in 8,921 villages, opened 2,560 Sahaj Shiksha Centres covering 47,000 children and started 529 new primary schools and 268 upper primary schools. The programme has also strengthened 239 pre-school centres of anganwadis and formed over 7,600 Mahila Groups.

Mahila Samakhya

Another externally-assisted programme with a specific focus on gender is Mahila Samakhya, started in 1989 in five States. It aims to promote women's education and empowerment of women in rural areas, particularly women in socially and economically marginalised groups. It endeavours to create a learning environment where women can collectively affirm their potential, gain and strength to demand information and knowledge, and move forward to change and take charge of their lives. Mahila Samakhya has reached the poor and marginal women who have been able to overcome social barriers and are addressing issues such as child marriage, child labour, and violence against women. A pool of aware women has been created through the Mahila Shikshan Kendras and there is an ever-increasing demand for literacy and education for their daughters and granddaughters. This has had a beneficial social impact like delaying the age of marriage of girls. The programme is currently implemented in over 9,000 villages in 53 districts spread over ten states.

Mid-Day Meal Scheme

The National Programme of Nutritional Support to Primary Education commonly known as the Mid-day Meal programme was launched in 1995. It aims to give a boost to universalisation of primary education by increasing enrolment, retention and attendance and simultaneously improving the nutritional status of students in primary classes. Under the scheme, cooked meals are served with calorie value equivalent to 100 gm of wheat or rice per student per school day. The honour of starting the Mid-day Meal scheme in elementary schools in the country goes to Tamil Nadu.

Mid-day Meal Scheme in Tamil Nadu

The Mid-day Meal Scheme in Tamil Nadu was started on a humble scale way back in 1925-26 by the Corporation of Madras with the aim to improve school attendance. Subsequently, philanthropists and voluntary organisations were urged to start free school lunch centres in villages and towns all over the state. In July 1956, the school lunch programme was launched as a 'people's movement' for organised charity as part of the 'School Improvement Efforts'. Impressed by the public response, the Government of Tamil Nadu (erstwhile Madras) took up the school lunch programme in 1957 and issued detailed rules for running the programme, which have been revised several times since then. In year 1961, the state started receiving CARE (Cooperative for American Relief Everywhere) food commodities for feeding 500,000 children through the school lunch programme. In 1978, 1.86 million children in 32,000 schools were covered and this number increased to 2.03 million in 33,306 schools in 1980-81.

The state achieved another milestone in 1982 with the launch of Nutritious Meal Programme for school children in classes Ist to Xth. This programme is being implemented through Nutritious Meal Centres located in schools and all children who are willing to enroll are fed. During 2001-02, 5.80 million children were enrolled for the Mid-day Meal Scheme.

The number of children covered under the programme has risen from 33.4 million in about 3,22,000 schools in 1995-96 to 105.1 million students in 7,92,000 schools spread over 576 districts in 2000-01. It is targeted to cover 107.2 million children in 578 districts during 2001-02. Over 15 lakh tonnes of foodgrains were lifted for the scheme during 2000-01 compared to 14 lakh tones in 1999-2000. Currently, only six states - Gujarat, Kerala, Orissa, Ṭamil Nadu, Chhattisgarh (174 tribal blocks) and Madhya Pradesh - and the Union Territory of Pondicherry are providing hot cooked meals under the programme. In Delhi, ready-to eat food is being distributed. The remaining states/ Union Territories are distributing foodgrains (wheat/rice). States like Himachal Pradesh, Kerala, Madhya Pradesh and Karnataka were able to lift 95.7 per cent, 92.9 per cent, 87.8 per cent and 86.6 per cent of foodgrains respectively under the scheme in 2000-01 while some others such as Arunachal Pradesh, Gujarat, Jharkhand and Delhi lifted only 12.78 per cent, 25.17 per cent, 30.33 per cent and 33.98 per cent foodgrains respectively.

The Mid-day Meal Scheme has been evaluated by different agencies at different points of time. The Operations Research Group, evaluated the scheme in July 1999 in ten states with the support of UNICEF and found that the scheme has attracted SC/ST children and children belonging to lower income groups to school. The Planning Commission also commissioned two studies in April 2000 to measure the impact of the scheme and found that a cooked meal programme was preferable not only from the health point of view but also because it attracted more children to schools. Similarly, other studies conducted by the National Council of Educational Research and Training (NCERT) and Public Report on Basic Education (PROBE) have also upheld the view that the scheme has had a positive impact in the direction of universalisation of primary education.

Despite the fact that the scheme has increased enrolment as well as retention of students, it has not been successful in achieving its ambitious targets for nation-wide coverage. Some of the weaknesses of the programme are:

- Non-provision of a cooked meal.
- Enrolment data, which is to be provided by the states each year and on the basis of which foodgrains are allocated for ten academic months, is not available. This is evident in the fact that there is a mismatch between the allocation and lifting of foodgrains.
- Inability of states to arrange the timely delivery of foodgrains. A major reason for this is the non-availability of funds with the implementing agencies to meet the initial expenditure on transportation charges, which is later reimbursed by the central government. This particularly affects schools in far-flung areas.
- Community participation in the implementation of the programme is lacking because of poor awareness and advocacy, among other things.
- Since the initial arrangement for Management Information System (MIS) through the National Informatics Centre NET (NICNET) did not take off, close monitoring and supervision of the programme was negligible, resulting in furnishing of erratic reports on utilisation as well as beneficiaries covered under the scheme.

Non-Formal Education (NFE) and EGS and AIE

The scheme of non-formal education (NFE), introduced in 1977-78 on a pilot basis and expanded in subsequent years, focused on out-of school children in the 6-14 age group who have remained outside the formal system due to socio-economic and cultural reasons. The scheme was initially limited to ten educationally backward states, covering urban slums, hilly, tribal and desert areas. The scheme has many lacunae – lack of enthusiasm of teachers, poor quality of training, ambiguity in curriculum and textbooks, lack of community participation, weak management system, insufficient outlay, a lack of emphasis on mainstreaming, etc. Moreover, most NFE centres were in habitations already served by formal schools.

The programme was revised and renamed the Education Guarantee Scheme and Alternative and Innovative Education (EGS & AIE) in 2000. It provided for opening EGS schools in habitations where there are no schools within a radius of 1 km. The EGS&AIE scheme will support diversified strategies for out-of-school children including bridge courses, back-to-school camps, seasonal hostels, summer camps, mobile teachers and remedial coaching. The investment cost per child per year has been increased from Rs. 375 to Rs. 845 at the primary level centre and from Rs. 580 to Rs. 1,200 at the upper primary level.

Janshala (GOI-UN) Programme

The Janshala (GOI-UN) Programme is a collaborative effort of the Government of India (GOI) and five United Nations (UN) agencies – UN Development Programme (UNDP), UNICEF, UN Economic and Social Commission (UNESCO), International Labour Organisation (ILO) and UNFPA. It provides programme support to the on-going efforts towards achieving UEE. UNDP, UNICEF and UNFPA have committed to contribute $ 20 million for the programme while UNESCO and ILO have offered technical know-how. Janshala is a community-based primary education programme that aims to make primary education more accessible and effective, especially for girls and children in deprived communities, marginalised groups, SCs/STs, minorities, working children and children with special needs. The programme covers 39 blocks in nine states—Andhra Pradesh, Jharkhand, Karnataka, Madhya Pradesh, Chhattisgarh, Maharashtra, Orissa, Rajasthan and Uttar Pradesh—with a total project outlay of Rs. 103.29 crore. The programme is to run for five years, from 1998 to 2002. At the state level, the programme is implemented through existing structures of educational administration. Janshala has started a large number of alternative schools in small and remote habitations in the programme areas, besides evolving strategies and setting up schools with community participation in the urban slums of Jaipur, Hyderabad, Ajmer, Bharatpur, Puri and Lucknow. Other major areas of achievement are in teacher training, multi-grade teaching, intervention for education of the disabled, setting up of block and cluster resources centres and strengthening capacities at the state, district and block level.

Sarva Shiksha Abhiyan

The Sarva Shiksha Abhiyan was launched towards the end of the Ninth Plan to achieve the goal of UEE through a timebound integrated approach, in partnership with states. The programme, which aims to provide elementary education to all children in the 6-14 age group by 2010, is an effort to improve the performance of the school system and provide community-owned quality elementary education in the mission mode. It also envisages bridging of gender and social disparities at the elementary level. The Sarva Shiksha Abhiyan has a special focus on the educational needs of girls, SCs and STs and other children in difficult circumstances.

Objectives of Sarva Shiksha Abhiyan

- All children to be in schools, Education Guarantee Scheme centres, alternate schools, back-to-school camps by 2003;
- all children to complete five years of primary schooling by 2007;
- all children to complete eight years of schooling by 2010;
- focus on elementary education of satisfactory quality with emphasis on education for life;
- bridge all gender and social disparities at the primary stage by 2007 and at the upper primary level by 2010; and
- universal retention by 2010.

Under the programme, habitation plans, prepared after micro-planning, household surveys, school mapping and diagnostic studies, form the basis for the District Elementary Education Plans (DEEP). Funds released to states would be channelised to registered societies at the state level. The Sarva Shiksha Abhiyan is expected to accord the highest priority to community monitoring, transparency in programme planning and implementation of capacity building at all levels as also to the adoption of a mission approach by the mainstream Education Department functionaries. A National Mission for Sarva Shiksha Abhiyan was constituted in November 2000 with the Prime Minister as the Chairman and the Minister for Human Resource Development as Vice-Chairman.

The scheme is expected to absorb most of the existing programmes, including externally aided programmes, within its overall framework with the district as the unit of programme implementation. To make the approach totally holistic and convergent, efforts would be made to dovetail programme implementation at the district level with all other departments. This would include programmes for children in the 0-6 age group under the Department of Women and Child Development, sports-related interventions of the Ministry of Sports and Youth Affairs, establishment of public libraries under the Department of Culture and nutrition and health programmes of the Ministry of Health.

INNOVATIVE PROGRAMMES IN EDUCATION IN DIFFERENT STATES

Several state governments have designed innovative programmes to improve the quality of education in schools.

HEAD START

The Rajiv Gandhi State Mission in Madhya Pradesh has introduced a project on a pilot basis for using computers to improve the quality of teaching in rural elementary schools through indigenous customised educational software. The idea is to integrate the use of computers with classroom activities to improve the child's comprehension of difficult parts of each subject as well as to instill computer literacy. A syllabus mapping the difficult areas of learning has been developed and educational software on this for all subjects is being prepared for use in the academic year 2002-03.

Started in November 2000, 648 Head Start centres were operationalised in middle schools that have a primary section and serve as Jan Shiksha Kendras or school cluster resource centres for primary schools in a radius of 1 km. A total of 2,358 teachers have been given training in computer enabled education.

GYANKALASH

The District Primary Education Programme in Himachal Pradesh, in collaboration with All India Radio, Shimla, has started a 15-minute bi-weekly programme called Gyankalash to provide academic support to primary teachers. The programme helps in improving the teachers' access to the knowledge, especially those in the remote areas as it is impossible to reach them through conventional means.

In the first phase of Gyankalash, topics were identified and radio scripts developed in workshops organised for the purpose.

Resource persons, teacher educators from state and district level, practicing teachers in secondary and primary schools participated in the workshops.

In the next phase, teachers and students from government primary schools were involved in the production and broadcast of the spots.

In order to motivate teachers, certificates were given to teachers on the successful completion of the training under different phases of Gyankalash.

NALI KALI

The Nali Kali programme in Karnataka was introduced in privately managed schools in 1999. Under the programme, learning takes place in an interactive situation in accordance with age-wise competency. Children are divided into groups and they master one level of competency, then move to another group to learn the next level of competency. Children learn at their own pace and the move from one level of competency to another is not dependent on the whole group's learning achievement. All teaching-learning processes involve songs, games, survey, story telling and use of educational toys. This method effectively eliminates the formal system of roll calls, examination, promotions, ranking - all these now deemed unhealthy - at least between the of 5 and 14.

The financial performance of the elementary education sector during the Ninth Plan is summarised in Table 18.2.

GOALS, TARGETS AND STRATEGIES FOR THE TENTH PLAN

Goals and Targets

In the elementary education sector, the Sarva Shiksha Abhiyan is in place with clear focus and medium-term goals. The Tenth Plan targets in respect to elementary education are:

Universal Access

- All children in the 6-14 age group should have access to primary schools, upper primary schools or their alternatives within a walking distance of 1 km and 3 km respectively.

Table-18.2
The Financial Performance of the Elementary Education Sector During the Ninth Plan

Sub-sector	*Eight Plan (Expenditure)*		*Ninth Plan (Outlay)*		*Expenditure*					*Total Anticipated expenditure Ninth Plan*
	Rs. Crore	*% age*	*Rs. Crore*	*% age*	*1997-98*	*1998-99*	*1999-00*	*2000-01*	*2001-02*	
Elementary Education	4,006.55	47.0	16,369.59	65.7	2,234.94	2,749.83	2,851.97	3,117.39	3,569.16	14,523.29
Adult Education	7,18.14	8.4	630.39	2.5	78.85	72.29	87.08	108.16	174.00	520.38

Note : Percentage expenditure under Elementary Education and Adult Education during the Eighth Plan is expenditure under these sub-sectors expressed as percentage of total expenditure in the education sector. Similarly %age outlay under these sub-sectors during the Ninth Plan is outlays for these sub-sectors expressed as percentage of total outlay of the education sector.

Source: Report of the Mid-Term Appraisal of the Ninth Five Year Plan, Planning Commission Department of Elementary Education and Literacy.

- All children in the 3-6 age group must have universal access to early childhood care and education centres.
- Need-based expansion of upper primary education facilities, particularly for the disadvantaged sections. There should be one upper primary school for every two primary schools.
- All schools should have buildings, toilets, drinking water, electricity, playgrounds, blackboards and other basic facilities. There must be provision of one classroom for every teacher at the elementary stage.

Universal Enrolment

- Enrolment of all children in schools or alternative arrangements by 2003.
- All children to complete five years of primary schooling by 2007.

Universal Retention

- Universal retention in the primary stage by 2007.
- Dropout rate to be reduced to less than 10 per cent for grades VI-VIII by 2007.

Universal Achievement

Improve the quality of education in all respects (content and process) to ensure reasonable learning outcomes at the elementary level, especially in literacy, numerics and in life skills.

Equity

- Bridge all gender and social gaps in enrolment, retention and learning achievement in the primary stage by 2007 and reduce the gap to 5 per cent in the upper primary stage by 2007.
- Special interventions and strategies to include girls, SC/ST children, working children, children with special needs, urban deprived children, children from minority groups, children below the poverty line, migratory children and children in the hardest-to-reach groups.

STRATEGIES FOR UNIVERSALISATION OF ELEMENTARY EDUCATION

The strategies and interventions during the Tenth Plan will mainly be guided by three major considerations: *(a)* magnitude of the task; *(b)* present challenges; and *(c)* the existing administrative and policy framework and the one that will be in place during the Plan period.

Magnitude of the Task: The Working Group on Elementary and Adult Education for the Tenth Five-Year Plan has estimated that in order to achieve the goal of UEE by 2010, enrolment at the primary level needs to grow at an average annual growth rate of 1.12 per cent for boys and 4.16 per cent for girls during the Plan period. At the upper primary level, the growth rate must be 4.62 per cent for boys and 8.03 per cent for girls. The average growth rate for boys and girls taken together should be 2.51 per cent at the primary and 6.08 per cent at the upper primary levels. The year-wise estimated additional enrolment during the Plan period are given in the Table 18.3.

Present Challenges: Achieving the goal of UEE poses three main challenges: (i) access to basic education for the unreached segments and social groups; (ii) qualitative improvement in content and processes so as to raise learning achievements; and (iii) tackling high dropout and low retention rates in primary and upper primary schools.

Table-18.3
Year-wise Estimated Additional Enrolment

Year	*Additional Enrolment*					
	Primary (Grade I-V)			*Upper Primary (Grades VI-VIII)*		
	Boys	*Girls*	*Total*	*Boys*	*Girls*	*Total*
2002-03	0.67	2.01	2.68	1.14	1.44	2.58
2003-04	0.67	2.10	2.77	1.19	1.54	2.73
2004-05	0.67	2.18	2.85	1.25	1.67	2.92
2005-06	0.69	2.27	2.96	1.31	1.81	3.12
2006-07	0.69	2.37	3.06	1.37	1.95	3.32
Total	3.39	10.93	14.32	6.26	8.41	14.67

Administrative and Policy Framework: The administrative and policy framework needs to be guided by the following concerns.

- The national resolve to provide free and compulsory education of satisfactory quality to all children up to the age of 14 years, as stipulated in the National Policy on Education;

- The 93rd Constitutional amendment making the right to elementary education a fundamental right and enforcing it through necessary statutory measures; and
- The spirit of the 73rd and 74th Constitutional amendments setting the stage for greater decentralisation of power and a significantly enhanced role for local bodies, community organisations as well as voluntary agencies in the efforts towards UEE.

Given this backdrop, the Tenth Plan strategy for achieving UEE must have the following salient features:

Holistic and Convergent Approach: As the existing policies and programmes are either for specific target groups/regions, there is need for an all-comprehensive programme covering the entire country. The Sarva Shiksha Abhiyan is such a programme and will be the main vehicle for achieving the goals of UEE.

Community Participation in UEE Programmes: The involvement of the community will be made more systematic by involving the Panchayati Raj Institutions (PRIs) and urban local bodies. Further down the hierarchy, VECs, Mother-Teacher Associations (MTA) and Parent-Teacher Associations (PTA) would have a formal role in the management of schools in the village.

Target-Groups Oriented Strategy: The Tenth Plan will lay emphasis on identifying the problem areas and formulating a separate strategy for each area, under the overall umbrella of the Sarva Shiksha Abhiyan. There will be special focus on children who have never enrolled or those who have droppedout without completing eight years of elementary schooling. Specific strategies would be devised for the difficult-to-reach groups in order to ascertain the reasons for their staying away from school system and to take steps to provide them quality elementary education.

Programmes for Achieving UEE

The following schemes would be the instruments by which these strategies would be translated into action during the Tenth Plan. Scheme-wise break-up of the Tenth Plan outlay is given in the Appendix.

Sarva Shiksha Abhiyan : Out of the approximately 207.76 million children in the 6-14 age group in 2000, the number of children not attending the schools is 40 million. Those outside the school system are mostly girls, SCs/STs children, working children, urban deprived children, disabled children and children in difficult circumstances. Providing access and motivation to these difficult to reach groups, without compromising on the quality of education, would be the challenge that the Sarva Shiksha Abhiyan would tackle in the Tenth Plan.

The Sarva Shiksha Abhiyan will totally subsume all existing programmes, barring the Mid-day Meals Scheme, and the scheme of Restructuring and Reorganisation of Teachers' Education. All legal agreements regarding externally-aide projects such as Mahila Samakhya, DPEP, Lok Jumbish, Shiksha Karmi, etc., will continue to apply unless specific modifications have been made in consultation with the funding agencies. In order to achieve a holistic and convergent approach, efforts would be made to dovetail programme implementation at the district level with all other programmes. This would include programmes for children in the 0-6 age group under the Department of Women and Child Development, sports-related interventions of the Department of Sports and Youth Affairs, establishment of public libraries under the Department of Culture, nutrition and school health programmes of the Ministry of Health and the employment generation/poverty alleviation programmes of Ministry of Rural Development. This dovetailing exercise would be undertaken while formulating the DEEPs.

Gender-Specific Programmes : The Tenth Plan would also rely on some women-centric programmes such as the existing Mahila Samakhya, and two new schemes, the Kasturba Gandhi Swantantra Vidyalaya (KGSV) and the National Programme for the Education of Girls at the Elementary Level (NPEGEL). Mahila Samakhya will be expanded both in terms of geographical reach and activities like the Mahila Shikshan Kendras. However, it will retain its objectives, identity and non-negotiable principles.

The KGSV and the NPEGEL are proposed to be taken up during the Tenth Plan, with the following features:

substantial number of primary schools without these facilities. The main thrust in the Tenth Plan should be to ascertain that all the primary schools have *pucca* buildings with all supporting infrastructural facilities.

Teachers Education

Improving the performance of teachers is the most important challenge in elementary education as they are the principal instruments of education. Besides, teachers' salary claims the major share of the state education budget. Although a lot has already been done to improve the quality of teachers, historical deficiencies in teachers' education and training has resulted in many of them having little understanding of the material they teach, poor teaching skills and poor motivation levels.

Besides addressing the issue of quality, the Tenth Plan would also place an exclusive emphasis on teacher education. Some of the broad strategies, which would be followed, are:

Development and strengthening of teacher education institutes

The focus of teacher education would be on the development of the following institutions:

- *District Institute of Education and Training (DIETs)* : Each state would be encouraged to rethink the structure of its DIETs as per needs of the district and effectiveness of the institution. Each DIET would be encouraged to draw up a development plan for itself, defining its role and setting goals for itself. Special attention will be paid to the development of libraries in DIETs, as well as providing computer facilities (including computer literacy training), exposure visits, networking and sharing among DIETs and other academic institutions on professional issues and the establishment of district resource groups. Further, new DIETs would be set up only in those states where the existing ones are functional and steps are taken to improve sub-standard DIETs.
- *College of Teacher Education (CTEs) and Institutes of Advanced Studies in Education (IASEs)* : The need for CTEs and IASEs in each state would be ascertained in terms of the needs for secondary teacher education and identified institutions would be strengthened. The identified CTEs/ IASEs would

need to prepare their individual plan of development, mentioning the areas in which they need to be strengthened and make a need assessment survey in the areas of their jurisdiction. They must also develop schedules and materials of inservice teacher training to cover secondary teachers and implement the National Council of Teacher Education (NCTE) project on imparting information technology (IT) literacy to the teachers. IASEs would be encouraged to play a greater role in elementary education and education of teacher educators.

- *Strengthening of State Councils for Educational Research and Training (SCERTs) :* The SCERT is identified as a key area for teacher education in the Tenth Plan. The state governments need to fulfill some essential conditions for being eligible for funds for strengthening of SCERTs, such as recruitment of appropriate faculty, linkage to DIETs, resource centres and schools, autonomy of SCERTs and proper maintenance of buildings, etc. Only then would the central government fund capacity building and training of SCERT faculty, development of infrastructure, computers and IT literacy programmes and hostels for residential training programmes, etc. SCERTs should be equipped to plan for computer education curricula, teacher training, etc., at the school level, strengthening of cells for teaching of English language at the elementary level, strengthening of pre-service education, etc., pre-service as well as In-service Training of Teachers, including Para-Teachers.

Professional Development of Teachers

The focus in the Tenth Plan would be on:

- Ensuring pre-service training to all elementary school teachers so that all untrained teachers can be trained within a period of three years, including through the distance learning mode.
- Enhancing pre-service training facilities in selected districts where the present capacity is not adequate.
- Improving the quality of elementary teacher pre-service education.
- Extending the provision of pre-primary teacher training by

strengthening existing institutions that provide, or are willing to provide, pre-service education for the preprimary stage.

- Developing specialised correspondence courses, of two months to one year's duration, for elementary teachers in collaboration with open universities, higher education institutions, good IASEs, NGOs with experience in quality education, and other professional organisations.
- Development of courses for in-service education of teachers that will carry credits and linking these to promotions and benefits.

Strengthening of Block Resource Centres (BRCs) and Cluster Resource Centres (CRCs)

With an emphasis on providing academic support to the teachers locally, depending on context-specific needs, DIETs would have close linkage with BRCs and CRCs whose personnel get academic support from them.

Professional Development of Practitioners, i.e. Teacher Educators, Managers and Others

New courses for teacher educators and curriculum developers would be developed and tried out on a pilot basis. Innovations and pilot projects in pre-service and in-service teacher education will be supported. Another major focus area would be networking of teacher education institutions and strengthening of teacher education by expanding access to digital resources. The networked institutions would then be able to use the Information and Communication Technologies (ICT) for online sharing of resources and for breaking the isolation of institutions.

Systematic Learner Evaluation

A mechanism for regular learner assessment will be designed and put in place to evaluate the impact and efficacy of measures taken for improvement in school quality.

Strategy for Dropouts

A large number of children dropout of school because of reasons relating to the school environment. These include attitude of teachers, irrelevant curriculum, sub-standard and uninteresting teaching, teacher absenteeism, corporal punishment, poor school infrastructure, inability to cope with the pace of learning, lack of parental support in the case of first generation learners, maladjustment, etc. Girls form the majority of the dropouts in all categories. The National Family Health Survey-II (NFHS-II), conducted in 1998-99, also observed that the main reasons for students droppingout include their not being interested in studies, the high private cost of education and the need for them to work, whether in their own farms, business/households or outside. These reasons held true for 75 per cent of dropouts.

The main challenge for education authorities at the central, state and district levels is to: *(a)* improve the supply, quality and retention power of education, particularly in rural primary schools and in the unreached segments; and *(b)* introduce innovative methods of providing education to identified disadvantaged and difficult groups to suit their timing and interests. The focus in the Tenth Plan would, therefore, be on pedagogic improvement and adoption of child-centered methods, which have been developed in programmes like DPEP; and building a positive environment that would include more attractive classroom designs, local contextual curriculum and more friendly evaluation techniques. Apart from a number of steps undertaken under the Sarva Shiksha Abhiyan to reduce the private cost of education, an incentive scheme linked to attendance has been suggested for girls, SCs/STs and poor children.

Where the children are droppingout because of the need to work, the emphasis would be on involving the community in motivating the parents to bring their children back to school so that they are in a position to complete eight years of elementary education. For those children who have already dropped out, suitable alternative education systems such as bridge courses, remedial teaching, back to school camps, etc., would be provided so that they can be mainstreamed into the formal system.

Strategy for Early Childhood Care and Education (ECCE)

Early childhood development is globally acknowledged as a significant input for lifelong development and successful completion of primary education. The Tenth Plan acknowledges ECCE as the first step in the education ladder. The major provider of ECCE is the

Integrated Child Development Services (ICDS) scheme which covers 15.8 million children (17.8 per cent of the child population of 3-6 years) through about 5,20,000 anganwadis in 35 states and Union Territories. Early Childhood Education or Pre-School Education is among the six components of the ICDS scheme and is one of its weakest. The Sarva Shiksha Abhiyan aims to support *(i)* strengthening the pre-school component in ICDS by need-based training of anganwadi sevikas, provision of learning materials, etc; *(ii)* setting up balwadis as pre-school centres in uncovered areas; *(iii)* building advocacy on the importance of early child development; *(iv)* organising training programmes for community leaders; *(v)* providing for intensive planning for ECCE; *(vi)* development of materials; and *(vii)* romoting convergence between the school system and the ECCE.

Community Participation in Elementary Education

Decentralisation provides a clear correlation between the needs of people and the steps taken by the Government to meet these demands. Planning from below and contextualised resource allocation for basic services would not only be more cost effective and produce better results but will also ensure that the quality of the services is directly proportional to the degree of community control and supervision. People's participation in the provision of basic services can, as mentioned in the Mid-Term Appraisal of the Ninth Five-Year Plan, contribute to the achievement of four main objectives, i.e. effectiveness, efficiency, empowerment and equity.

The thrust on decentralised planning and management came as early as in 1986, in the National Policy of Education, which had proposed decentralisation as a fundamental requirement for improving the efficiency and effectiveness of educational planning and management and for evolving a meaningful framework for accountability. The Approach Paper to the Tenth Five-Year Plan has also reiterated that the mere establishment of schools and hiring of teachers will not lead to an improvement in education if teachers remain absent, as is common, especially in the rural areas. It is, therefore, essential that control over schools and teachers should be transferred to local bodies, which have a direct interest in teacher performance. Planning, supervision and management of education would have to be through local bodies at the district, block and village levels. Efforts should also be made for the social mobilisation of local communities for adult literacy campaigns and for the promotion of primary education.

While the decentralisation of governance, through the 73rd and 74th Constitutional amendments, has facilitated the transfer of the management of schools to panchayats/local bodies, the real challenge now is to create an enabling environment for the qualitative participation of all groups. The qualitative participation should mean that the community is able to have a voice and exercise its choice. It also involves the development of human, organisational and management capacity to solve problems and sustain the improvements.

Recognising the fact that community participation is the surest way to ensure UEE and improve the quality of education, several state governments have already initiated the process of decentralising the management of elementary education by involving the community. Other states would also be encouraged to transfer the management of primary schools to panchayat/local bodies with special emphasis on:

- Encouraging community participation in promoting enrolment, retention and other aspects of education. PRIs and grass root level organisations like VECs, PTAs, MTAs, etc. should become the vehicles of community mobilisation;
- Evolving a community-based monitoring system evolved with full transparency;
- Making community mobilisation through intensive micro-planning and school mapping mandatory; and
- Participatory implementation of goals and strategies.

This shift in planning and management strategy will also require a massive effort to train and continually support educational bodies set up under the PRIs/urban local bodies. There is an urgent need to reorient the outlook of government functionaries and their perception of their roles. Efforts will be made to reorient the programmes of various resource institutions at the national and state levels to meet these requirements. Towards this end, the local level institutions in education and allied sectors will be strengthened adequately. Besides, it is envisaged that distance education mechanisms will be suitably strengthened and reoriented to play a significant role in the task of building capacities among local-level functionaries.

Pursuing the goal of decentralisation, along with partnership between the Centre and the States, demands careful orchestration of polices and programmes, particularly in the area of elementary education. As envisaged in the National Policy on Education, and subsequently reiterated by several bodies, the central government and its institutions will continue to play a major role both for coordination and capacity building. It will continue to monitor the progress of attaining national goals in the field of elementary education.

Synergetic Partnership with the Private Sector

The task of providing basic education in a country with diverse conditions is so stupendous that it is difficult to expect the government sector alone to do this effectively. Even though private initiatives have always been a part of the school education endeavour, it has neither been large nor of a sizeable magnitude in the efforts to universalise elementary education. The private sector can contribute not only in monetary and material terms, but also in the form of expertise for improving quality through effective management of the system and the development of locally relevant teachinglearning materials. Some efforts in this direction have already been made by many states including Karnataka, which has a school adoption scheme. More collaborative efforts at the institutional level as well as in programme implementation will be designed to expand the role of private initiatives in elementary education. A synergetic public-private partnership would be built up during the Tenth Plan to achieve the objective of UEE. Specifically, the following measures would be encouraged:

- More collaborative efforts with the private sector and expansion of the role of private initiatives.
- Improve the functioning of government schools in partnership with the private sector, within the broad parameters of state policy.
- Provide support to initiatives introduced by private schools for deprived children.
- Encourage the opening of private schools, without compromising on quality.
- Provide computer education to children, utilising the expertise and resources of the private sector.

Convergence as a Strategy for Optimum Utilisation of Resources

Cost effectiveness and efficiency in the delivery of services under various educational programmes, which are mostly affected by the socio-economic and political conditions, can have a far-reaching impact on the most important determinant of development, i.e. human capital formation. Effectiveness of the delivery of services in the social sector also needs a high degree of integration and convergence in the planning and implementation of programmes of related social sectors. Services like literacy, elementary education, primary health care, nutrition, mother and childcare, family welfare and rural development have strong linkages and can only be strengthened through an appropriate integrated approach which will optimise public expenditure and reinforce the effective delivery system. All efforts would be made in the Tenth Plan to achieve convergence both in the formulation of schemes/programmes as well as in their implementation through effective coordination at the national/state level and lower levels of administration.

THE PATH AHEAD

Education has an intrinsic value for the development of the society and helps in the achievement of a better social order. Greater literacy and basic education help individuals to make better use of available economic opportunities. The Government has decided to make free and compulsory elementary education a fundamental right.

The Government has taken a major initiative by launching the Sarva Shiksha Abhiyan, which aims at universalisation of elementary education within a given time frame, in partnership with states. However, it will have to be ensured that there is no compromise on quality. In fact, the lessons learnt from all the successful programmes on literacy should be made an integral part of the Sarva Shiksha Abhiyan on a continuous basis.

The implementation of the Sarva Shiksha Abhiyan will result in a significant increase in the number of children completing elementary education. This will simultaneously increase the demand for secondary education. This aspect has to be dovetailed in the planning for education and steps have to be taken to gradually strengthen the secondary schools along with other facilities to keep pace with the increased demand.

It is important that the Centre make adequate provision of funds for the fulfilment of the objectives of the Sarva Shiksha Abhiyan and this has to be backed by a complementary on the part of the states. Needless to say, the programme cannot succeed without proper utilisation of the available funds. Effective methods have to be evolved to transfer responsibility for funds and personnel to PRIs so as to assign greater role to them as envisaged in the Constitution.

Systematic mobilisation of the community and creation of an effective system of decentralised decision-making are essential pre-requisites for the achievement of the objectives of the Sarva Shiksha Abhiyan. This involves the cooperation of all stakeholders - the central government, the states, local government bodies, teachers, parents, NGOs, academic institutions and the children themselves. There is also a need for capacity building at all levels to make the programme self-sustainable. The implementation of the Sarva Shiksha Abhiyan with the involvement of all the stakeholders must ultimately result in a transparent and broad-based system of education.

Finally, the need to impart value-based education to the children at the early stages of schooling can hardly be overemphasised. The essential elements of such education should be based on the development of concern towards the needs of society and the nation among the children. In this contemporary world, the value should also be based on the functional utility of education and should highlight the dignity of labour. The idea of creation of wealth should be incorporated into the education system.

REFERENCE

1. Government of India, *Elementary Education*—Tenth Five Year Plan 2002-2007.

APPENDIX

MODEL QUESTION PAPER-I

Essay Type Questions

1. Compare the views of Gandhiji and Dewey on early childhood education.
2. Assess the state of early childhood education in India. What are the shortcomings that you have observed? Suggest measures for improvement.
3. Explain the recent trends and developments in early childhood education in UK and USA. Critically examine their influence on theory and practice of early childhood education in India.
4. Bring out the influence of home and community in the personality development of the individual during early childhood.

Paragraph Type Questions

5. What do you mean by compensatory education?
6. Bring out the salient features of Froebel's Kindergarten system
7. What type of child guidance programme do you envisage to deal with the maladjustment behaviour problems of children?
8. Trace the origin and development of pre-school education in Kerala?
9. How would you cater to the needs of gifted children?
10. Name the important emotions commonly found in pre-

school. children. What are the characteristics of childhood emotions?

11. Mention the stages of cognitive development in children according to Piaget. Explain the salient features of cognitive development in each stage.
12. How are concepts formed in children? Mention the stages. Illustrate.
13. In what ways do a knowledge of educational psychology benefit the pre-school teacher?
14. Montessori introduced several innovative measures in early childhood education. – explain.
15. Examine the factors that influence language development in pre-school children.
16. Illustrate with examples, how parent-teacher cooperation will help the spontaneous development of children in the early childhood stage.
17. As a pre-school teacher, explain how you will provide science experiences to pre-school children.
18. Children in the early childhood stage enjoy hearing stories from teachers, parents and grand-parents. Explain the role of story telling in the mental development of the child.
19. Child psychologists often remark that today's children are too much subjected to formal learning, depriving of their opportunity to play. Do you agree with this remark? If so, give you suggestions to solve this problem.
20. What are the important methods of child study? Explain any *two*.

MODEL QUESTION PAPER – II

Essay Type Questions

1. Explain how child rearing practices influence the mental make-up of the child.
2. Discuss the role of "Home" on child development and learning.
3. Briefly outline any *two* theories of learning and how they are relevant to pre-school education.
4. "Children learn more imitation than by reasoning"- Discuss.

Paragraph Type Questions

5. Outline the contribution of Froebel towards childhood education.
6. Mention *five* conditions that prevail in modern homes which are *not* conducive for children's education.
7. Can we condition children to behave in a particular way? Is it good or bad?
8. What is learning by insight? Can it be used in childhood education?
9. How are picture puzzles useful in a pre-school?
10. "The story bridges the gap between the child and the world" How?
11. How will you provide number experiences to pre-school children?
12. List the minimum essential equipment needed for a pre-school.
13. "To-day's agencies of early childhood education are more commercial in out-look than educational" – Comment.
14. How will you identify gifted children in a pre-school?
15. How will you cater to the needs of slow learning children?
16. Discuss the role of "Drama" as a socializing activity.
17. Mention any *five* stories and songs which can be used to instill moral values in children.
18. Explain the theory of surplus energy as related to children's activities.
19. Mention any *five* essential qualities of a good pre-school teacher.
20. When should we repremand children? Is it good or bad?

MODEL QUESTION PAPER -III

Essay Type Questions

1. Explain the recent trends and developments in Early Childhood Education in U.K. and U.S.A. Critically examine their influence on theory and practice of Early Childhood Education in India.
2. Given an estimate of the different phases of development during childhood. How can this information be exploited for organising effective programme of Early Childhood Education? Give examples.
3. Explain in what way the early child rearing practices influence the mental make-up of children in future.
4. What is meant by "maladjustment in children". Analyse two problems of this kind bringing out their symptoms, possible causes, remedial and preventive measures.

Paragraph Type Questions

5. Explain the need for early childhood education.
6. How do pre-school children develop number concepts?
7. What are Forebel's gifts to pre-school children?
8. What is learning readiness? How will you promote this in pre-school children?
9. Which stage of Piaget's theory of cognitive development is more applicable at the pre-school level? Why?
10. "The story bridges the gap between the child and the world." How?
11. Give and account of the records to be maintained in a pre-school and classify them on the basis of the purpose they serve.
12. How far is the pre-school and extension of the home?
13. Do you consider that today's children are subjected to "play deprivation". If so, give suggestions to solve this problem.
14. Describe any one language game suitable for pre-school children.
15. State the principles one should bear in mind in planning the educational activities during early childhood.
16. As a pre-school teacher, how will you provide science experiences to pre-school children.
17. How would you apply the principles of mental hygiene to Early Childhood Education?

18. Give a brief write-up about the work of agencies involved in the early childhood education in Kerala.
19. Briefly assess the ideas of Dewey of Early Childhood Education.
20. How would you cater to the needs of gifted children?

MODEL QUESTION PAPER – IV

Essay Type Questions

1. What are the various methods generally adopted in child study? Describe how you would use any one of these methods to study the pre-school children.
2. Discuss the contribution of Montessori and Gandhiji for early childhood education.
3. Make a critical appraisal of the functioning of pre-school education in Kerala with reference to curriculum and administration.
4. Describe the mental and social development of Pre-school children.
5. Explain the concept "Compensatory education" and describe how it could be given in the pre-primary and primary schools.
6. Explain the role of home and community in the personality development of children.
7. What could be the cause for maladjustment in primary school children? What type of guidance would you offer such children in schools?
8. Suggest in broad outlines a curriculum for Pre-school education in India.

Paragraph Type Questions

9. Explain the need for early childhood education.
10. Comment on the applicability of Rousseau's negative education to pre-primary and primary stages.
11. State some of the landmarks in the history of pre-school education in England.
12. How do pre-school children develop number concepts?
13. State some of the behaviour problems that pre-school children present to the teacher and explain how as a teacher you would deal with any one of them.
14. Explain the egocentric and socialised aspects of children's oral language.
15. Suggest a list of aids that a pre-school institution should possess
16. What are Froebel's gifts to pre-school children?
17. What are the agencies conducting pre-school education in India? Comment on the curriculum that some of these agencies are following.
18. What is learning readiness relating to reading and writing?

MODEL QUESTION PAPER – V

Essay Type Questions

1. Explain Piaget's theory in respect of the development of language and the mathematical and scientific concept in children.
2. Give an estimate of the different phases of development during childhood. How can this information be exploited for organising effective programme of early childhood education? Give example.
3. Describe the recent trends and developments in pre-school education in the U.K. and the U.S.A. What is their influence on theory and practice of early childhood education in India?
4. Discuss briefly the various methods of child study bringing out clearly their efficacy in early childhood.

Paragraph Type Questions

5. Explain the concept of compensatory education.
6. Mention the dominant ideas underlying Froebel's Kindergarten.
7. "The story bridges the gap between the child and the world" How?
8. Do you consider that today's children are subjected to "Play depreivation". If so, give suggestions to solve this problem.
9. As a pre-school teacher, how will you provide science experiences to pre-school children.
10. Describe the concept of development task with regard to the stage related to early childhood.
11. What is giftedness? How can it be identified in children?
12. How would the maintenance of the cumulative record help the cause of early childhood education.
13. Describe any one cognitive activity suitable for pre-school children.
14. Having learnt the philosophy and principles of early childhood education, how would you organise a kindergarten in your area?
15. Indicate how the child rearing practices at home influence the development of personality in children.
16. State the views of Gandhiji on early childhood education.

17. Briefly assess the ideas of Dewey on early childhood education.
18. How does Bruner explain individual differences in mental ability among young children?
19. Briefly explain the concept of learning readiness.
20. What factors led to maladjustment?

MODEL QUESTION PAPERS - VI

Essay Type Questions

1. Trace the origin and development of pre-school education in any one advanced country. In the light of the above, offer suggestions for improving the provisions of pre-school education in our country.
2. State briefly the common behaviour problems of pre-school children and suggest certain possible ways to tackle these problems.
3. Discuss the important aspects of Universalisation of Elementary Education. Examine how far India has achieved this target.
4. Can we justify the placement of education in the Concurrent List? What are the constitutional provisions for giving education to all?

Paragraph Type Questions

5. Mention the conditions that prevail in modern which are not conducive for the development of children at elementary level.
6. What are the characteristics of childhood emotions? Name the important emotions commonly found in pre-school children.
7. In what ways do a knowledge of educational psychology benefit the pre-school teacher?
8. Mention the various activities entrusted to DIET.
9. Discuss the role of "Drama" as a socialising activity.
10. Which stage of Piaget's theory of cognitive development is more applicable at the pre-school level? Why?
11. Discuss the principles one should bear in mind in planning educational activities for elementary school children.
12. How will you as a teacher in primary school cater to the needs of gifted and backward children?
13. What is the role of SCERT in improving the quality of education in our state?
14. Describe the concept of developmental task with regard to the stage related to elementary.
15. Mention the dominant ideas underlying Froebel's Kindergarten.

16. Examine the role of story telling in the mental development of the child.
17. "Today's agencies of elementary education are more commercial in okutlook than educational." Comment.
18. Do you consider that today's children are subjected to "play deprivation".

BIBLIOGRAPHY

A Curriculum for the Pre-school Child Learning to Learn – Audrey Curtis

Abbasi, P. (2004). *Elementary School Facilities in India and Iran.* Edutracks.

Abhimanyu Singh (Elementary Education) – *Fifty Years of Elementary Education*, Department of Education, Government of India.

Aggarwal, J.C. (2003). *Development and Planning of Modern Education.* New Delhi: Vikas Publishing House (P.) Ltd.

Arora, G.L. Singh Ajit, Yadav SK and Yadav DD (1996). *Recurrent Training of Primary School Teachers.* Resource Persons at Cluster, Block and District Levels. New Delhi, NCERT (Mimeo).

Austin, Gilbert R. *Early Childhood Education.* An International Perspective, New York: Academic Press, 1976.

Banta, T. (1966). *Is these Really a Montessori Method?* Columbus, Ohio: Ohio Psychological Association and Ohio Psychiatric Association.

Bloom, Benjamin, S. (1964). *Stability and Change in Human Characteristics.* New York: John Wiley & Sons Inc.

Bowers, J. Howard and Burkett, Charles W. (1988). "Physical Environment Influences Related to Student Achievement, Health. Attendance, and Behaviour". CEFPI Journal, 26(4), 33-34.

Brown, G. (1977). *Child Development.* London: Open Books, Central Advisory Board of Education (CABE). Pre-Primary Education (Chapter II). In Post-War Development in India – A Report, Govt. of India.

Burnett, Bumett, G. (1995). *Overcrowding in Urban Schools.* ERIC Clearing house on Urban Education (ERIC/CUE Digest Number 107). www.ERIC.ORG.

Butts, R. Freeman. (1955). *A Cultural History of Western Education.* New York: Mc Graw-Hill Book, Co., Inc.

Cervantes, R.P. (1999). *The condition of school facilities as related to student academic achievement and behavior.* Thesis (Ed.D.)–University of Alabama.

Chaube, S.P. & Chaube, A. (1987). *Foundations of Education.* New Delhi: Vikas Publishing House (P.) Ltd.

Child Development - Laura E. Berk.

Child Development-Issues, Policies and Programmes Vol. I, II & III-Dolly Singh

Cole, Luella. (1950). *A History of Education-Socrates to Montessori.* New York: Holt Rinehart and Co.

Constitution Amendment in India – by Dr. R.C. Bhardwaj

Constitution of India – by C.K. Jain

Daresh, John, C. (1987). *Research Trends Staff Development and In-service Education. Journal of Education for Teaching,* 13(1). 3-11.

Department of Education and Science (1989). *School Teacher Appraisal-* A National Framework. Report of the National Steering Group on the School Teacher Appraisal, Pilot Study, MHSO, London.

Department of Education and Science, Britain, Low-Cost Day Provision for the Underfives, 197.

Early Childhood Care and Education – Mohante.

Early Childhood Care and Education – U.K. Rao.

Educational Policies Commission, *Universal Opportunities for Early Childhood Education, Washington,* D.C., Govt. Printing Office, 1966.

Eva L. Essa, *Introduction to Early Childhood Education* (3rd Ed.).

Evans, Ellis D. (1975). *Contemporary Influence in Early Childhood Education,* New York: Holt Rinehart and Winston, Inc.

Ganta, R. and Dash, B.N. (2005). *Foundations of Education.* Hyderabad: Neelkamal Publishers (P) Ltd.

Government of India Education Commission (1964-66). New Delhi.

Government of India Programme of Action, MHRD, New Delhi 1992.

Government of India, *District Institute of Education and Training: Guidelines*, MHRD, New Delhi, 1989.

Government of India, *Elementary Education*—Tenth Five Year Plan 2002-2007.

Government of India, *National Policy on Education*, MHRD, New Delhi, 1986.

Govt. of India, *Education and National Development the Report of Education Commission*, New Delhi: Manager of Publications, 1966. pp-149-151.

Grossnickle, Donald (1987). *In-service Follow-up. What to Do After the Expert Leaves*. NASSP Bulletin, March, 11-15.

Gupta, K.M. (1996). *Teachers' Performance in Mathematics and Reading Test-Indian Educational Review*, Vol. 3(1). 92-104.

Gupta, V.P., Sharma, H.K. and Bhattacarjee (1996). *Assessment of Training Needs of Primary Teachers in Language and Mathematics in DPEP Districts of Assam*. NCERT, Experiment (Underprint).

Innovations in Teaching-Learning Process—Chauhan S.S.

Introduction to Early Childhood Education—Jo Ann Brewer.

Issacs, S. (1929). *The Nursery Years*, London: Routledge and Kegan Paul.

Issacs, S. (1932). *The Children We Teach*, London: University of London Press.

Issacs, S. (1933). *Social Development in Young Children*, London: Routledge and Kegan Paul.

Jangira, N.K. Singh, Ajit and Yadav, S.K. (1994). *Training Needs and Motivation of Primary Teachers*. New Delhi: NCERT (Mimeo).

Joyce, B. and Showers. B. (1980). *Improving In-service Training: The Message of Research Educational Leadership*. Feb, pp. 379-385.

Katz, L. *Early Childhood Education as a Discipline*, Young Children, 1971, 26, 82.

Kaveeshwar, G.W. (Ed.), *Problems of Childhood Education in India. In The Report of All India Child Education Conference*, (Indore Report). Indore: Balaniketan Sangh, 1955.

MacDonald, James B. *A Proper Curriculum for Young Children*, Phi Delta Kappa 50, No. 7, (March 1969): 406.

Managing Behaviour Problems in Children—Reeta Peshwaria

Muralidharan, R. (Ed.) *Relating Pre-School to Primary School*, New Delhi: Indian Association of Pre-School Education.

Muralidharan, R., & Banerji, U. *A Guide for Nursery School Teachers*, New Delhi: NCERT, 1969.

Murty, S.K. (1992). *Contemporary Problems and Current Trends in Education*. Ludhiana: Parkash Brothers.

Nutrition, Education and Child Development—Anajali Patnaik.

Piaget, J. (1965). *The Child's Conception of Number*. W.W. Norton.

Pre-school Education—Bhooder Singh.

Primary Education—U.K. Singh & K.N. Sudarshan.

Primary Schooling in India—Amarjeet, Sinha.

Principles of Teaching in the Elementary Schools—Macomber.

Principles, Methods and Techniques of Teaching (2nd Ed.) —Aggarwal, J.C.

Rawat, D.S. (1970) *Pre-Primary Teacher Education Curriculum*. New Delhi: NCERT.

Research and Policy Committee of the Committee for Economic Development, Education for the Urban Disadvantaged From Pre-School to Employment, New York: Committee for Economic Development, 1971.

School Education in 1990's—NCERT Publication.

Singh, Ajit and Kumar, Anil (1996). *Training Needs of Primary School Teachers*, Indian Educational Review. 31(1), 83-91.

Studies in Teaching and Learning Self-evaluation for Primary Schools- I.A. Rodger & J.A.S. Richardson

Surgent, John (Sir), *Society, Schools and Progress in India*, Oxford: Pergamon Press, 1968.

Taneja, R.P. (2000). *Dictionary of Education*. Anmol Publishing Ltd.

Teacher and Education in Indian Society—by Dr. K.V. Eapen.

Teaching in the Early Years—Bernard Spodek.

Textbook on child Development—Rajammal P., N. Jaya Devadas.

The Developing Child—Helen Bee.

The Indian Express, Bombay, February 2, 1955.

The Years before School—Guiding Pre-school Children—Vivian Edmiston Todd, Helen Hefferman

UNESCO, *Education in Asia*, Bangkok, UNESCO Regional Office for Education in Asia, No. 5, March, 1974.

UNESCO, *New Approaches to Education of Children of Pre-School Age Report of a Regional Meeting of Experts*, Bangkok, UNESCO Regional Office for Education in Asia and Oceania, 1979.

UNESCO, *World Survey of Pre-School Education*, Paris: UNESCO, 1976.

Watkin, B.R. (1977). *Need Assessment Kits, Models and Tools.* Educational Technology, 17(2). 5-18.

Index